Praise for *College Baseball and Other Shenanigans*

"Bob shows excitement, fun and entertainment all around baseball, our national past time."

—WHITEY HERZOG,
Cardinals General Manager, HOF 2010

"Bob manages baseball and college days into an exciting, fun, enjoyable story."

—LEE THOMAS,
Special Assistant to the General Manager,
Baltimore Orioles and General Manager
of the Philadelphia Phillies, 1988-1997.

"Bob's college baseball story keeps the athletic trainer and the training room right in the middle of all the excitement."

—GENE GIESELMANN,
athletic trainer for St. Louis Cardinal Baseball,
1968-1997 (29 years)

"Including both baseball and shenanigans in the title is an accurate description of this humorous read! I learned some things about SIU's history that perhaps a chancellor shouldn't know!!!"

—DR. RITA HARTUNG CHENG,
Chancellor SIU Carbondale, 2010-2014

and OTHER
SHENANIGANS

and OTHER SHENANIGANS

Robert Hardcastle

College Baseball and Other Shenanigans

ISBN: 978-0-9908634-1-0

Cover Design and Interior Layout: AuthorSupport.com

This book is dedicated to God and to my parents, Ann Marie and Hubert Hardcastle; to Jan, my beautiful and wonderful wife of more than 50 years; my brother Tom; Jan's and my children, Jody and Scott; our grandchildren Jordan, Ally, David, Ashley, Rachel, and our great-grandson Evan.

I owe my life to them.

ACKNOWLEDGEMENTS

IN MOST BOOKS acknowledgements go to those people who have helped with the writing of the book. But, first, I want to acknowledge many more.

First, I'd like to thank all my baseball coaches. They include Percy Lumsden, Al Grosch, Earl Priestner, my high school baseball coach Ray Elliott and my college coach Glenn "Abe" Martin. My tennis coach, Don Dippold, also taught me about life in and out of sports.

To all my fellow baseball players, thank you. There have been so many fun times around the sport of baseball. To our 1956 Stockham Post American Legion National Championship teammates and coaches, Al Grosch and Earl Priestner: Thank you for the thrill of winning!

Throughout the years, I have found that playing baseball enabled me to go to college, get a good education, learn about life, start a business, and earn a living to support my family.

My thanks to our Delta Investments Team – Chris, Jay, Jan, Jody,

Mark, Barb, Marilyn, Suzanne, and Tiffany for doing those things in the investment field that I can't do, don't want to do and won't do. They also covered me during times of stress, sickness and despair.

Thank you Southern Illinois University–Carbondale for providing me with four years of an athletic scholarship, an education that led to my two degrees, a bachelor's and a master's, a place to teach, and a community to start my business career. I want to express extra gratitude to Coach "Abe" Martin, who showed me that baseball is not everything; that living a good life, being a good person and enjoying your surroundings is worth much more than just winning the ballgame.

A big thank you to Barb Allen, my secretary, who spent hours typing my dictation, all the while thinking, "Oh Bob, you can't say that!"

A special thanks to consulting editor Katy Gurley, who took my words and put them in a way that allows you, the reader, to better see, hear and understand my story.

My special and enduring thanks to my parents, Annie and Hubert Hardcastle. My dad always says that he, a former deli owner, is still "a-cookin'" while my mother, Annie, a former cashier, is still "a-sellin.'"

I wrote this book so you could enjoy, through laughter and appreciation, how fun college days, sports and education were to me and, very likely were to you, too.

Enjoy!

Bob

TABLE OF CONTENTS

PROLOGUE

I STAND IN the right-handed batter's box; the bases are loaded. The pitcher looks in. I'm thinking: "Come on! What's it going to be? Fastball? Slider? Throw it in here." He winds up and throws. Here it comes, and I swing. It's deep! It's long! It's a grand slam homer as I clear the bases and run around the field. The crowd jumps to its feet, cheering, screaming and going wild....

I blink and slowly wake up. My alarm is buzzing. I reach over to turn it off and lie back against the pillows to think about my dream before it fades from my memory. I realize it is a dream I've had before. The dream is of baseball and times past, from hitting grounders when I was barely old enough to hold a bat to the ball fields of my college days.

This morning, I go into the bathroom and throw cold water on my face. It's time to wake up and go to work, where I am a successful financial guy with my own company, Delta Investments. But as I drive to the office, I can't shake the dream as I remember those days of playing ball when I was a freshman in college and how I, with a tenacity I was born with, set my sights on the majors.

CHAPTER ONE

A Burning Desire

THE FIRST THING I remember as a kid was my dad taking me out in the backyard to play catch. I was about seven. We lived in a 32-unit building and each apartment had a bit of a backyard. It was in our tiny backyard that my dad taught me how to catch the ball low with the glove fingers-down and turn the glove fingers up to catch a ball chest high or above. I learned to shag the ground balls he hit, and he taught me to hit ground balls to him. We had a big wooden fence that stretched all the way across the back of our apartment complex, and behind that was an alley. A fence on the other side ran across the backyard of the people who lived in houses across the alley. (With our tiny backyard, small apartment, and modest means, I always thought anybody who lived in a house was rich.) Anyway, we had plenty of room to hit the ball – or so we thought.

One day, we were hitting grounders,
and Tom threw the ball to me.
I fouled it off and it went straight up
behind me, busting our bathroom window.

Whack!

I only got in trouble twice while playing ball in the backyard. My brother, Tom, who was six years younger, would play catch with me and hit grounders. One day, Tom threw the ball to me, and I fouled it straight back into our bathroom window.

Another time I was hitting grounders to Tom, and I got underneath Tom's pitch and hit the ball like a shot. It went way over Tom's head, over our fence, across the alley, over the other fence, and towards a house and through the kitchen window, where an Italian lady was at the sink washing dishes. She came running out of the door with my ball, yelling and screaming in Italian. When my dad found out that I broke her window, I knew I would be in trouble that coming Friday, which was the day my father meted out the punishments.

A Shortstop for Life

I also started playing Indian ball, a locally originated game for a minimum of three players with no bases required, and a game called "bottle caps" in the alleys of North St. Louis when I was about 10 or 11 years old. In bottle caps, you played one-on-one with the pitcher, and it was big fun. The pitcher threw the bottle cap, and you hit it with a broomstick handle. When they threw the bottle cap flat, it would drop, rise, break in, and break out. You never knew what the bottle cap was going to do. Playing bottle caps gave you a great eye, because if you could hit the cap, you could easily hit a baseball. We'd play that in the alley almost every day. It's hard to play bottle caps now because the caps on the bottles today don't have any cork in them. The cork helped hold the caps aloft. Without the cork, the metal caps just fall to the ground.

Another game we played was corkball. Just like its name, you hit a small ball made of cork. I had so much fun playing these neighborhood games, I decided to try out for a summer baseball team and, at the age of 10 or so, got in. All I had was my glove, bat, and tennis shoes – and a burning desire to play.

One day, I ran the nine blocks from home to Fairgrounds Park in North St. Louis, where there were tryouts for a baseball team. The manager divided up the team and put me at shortstop. I caught the first baseball hit to me and threw the guy out. The first time I batted, I popped up to the second baseman. The second time I was up, I hit a double. I made a couple of plays at shortstop, and then after practice, the coach said, "Hardy, you've made the team. You're gonna be our shortstop."

So, from then on, I was a shortstop – all the way through high school and college – and beyond.

On a Roll: A National Championship, and a Scholarship

I played a lot of baseball with neighborhood kids. But I really got the bug for becoming a pro when I tried out for the Beaumont High School baseball team in St. Louis and got in.

> '*You always seemed to be in the right place*
> *at the right time – you weren't fancy, but you were*
> *a consistent player.' –* **Rogers Robinson.**

My good friend, Rogers Robinson, who would go on and play with the St. Louis Cardinals Minor Leagues Baseball for ten years, went to Central High School, Beaumont's rival. He remembers when ball players from

Central and Beaumont High Schools teamed up and become the Stockham Post American Legion Team. The team won the State Championship and then the National Championship in 1956. Robinson was the first black player – an outfielder – from those two schools to play on the Stockham Post Team. I was captain of the team, and as usual, I played shortstop.

"You always seemed to be at the right place at the right time," Rogers told me. "You weren't fancy, but you were a consistent player and very seldom made a mistake and showed leadership from the beginning. Everyone just knew you were going to go on and become successful."

He reminded me that when we won the National, we got to go to New York and be on "*The Today Show*" with Dave Garroway, the founding host and anchor. We also went to see the Yankees at Ebbets Field where St. Louisan Yogi Berra was playing.

'When you arrive at a fork in the road, take it.' – Yogi Berra

Because I played well during high school, a baseball coach, Coach Glen "Abe" Martin, from Southern Illinois University at Carbondale scouted me in several games by the time I was a senior in 1958-59. He thought I was a terrific player and eventually offered me a scholarship. With a tip of the hat to Yogi, my fork in the road was that I could have gone one direction – waited and applied to other schools – or another, which was Carbondale. The Carbondale scholarship offer was just too good to pass up. In addition, I received The Saluki Award.* That award paid for my books, fees, and tuition of $59.75 per quarter. The scholarship also paid for my room and board, 200 bucks a trimester – a lot in those days.

---

* A Saluki, an Egyptian dog, was SIU's mascot. The story goes that Salukis could run forever; they would run and run until the birds got so tired flying they'd finally drop to the ground. When they did, the Salukis would gobble them up and take them back to the king.

4

It was a working scholarship, where my job was to line the field, keep it intact and make sure all the equipment was clean, accounted for and ready to go. That was the deal.

My dear friend of 55 years, Bob Kurston, and I lived in the same neighborhood and practically grew up together. He remembers when I got my scholarship to Carbondale and says I haven't changed much since those early days (I'll take that as a compliment!).

"You are no different today than those early days when you showed up with a positive attitude toward everything. You were a profound achiever," he told me. Bob, who went into the Air Force after high school and later attended the University of Maryland, didn't play baseball, but lobbed tennis balls to me that I could hit. He was, and still is, one of my closest friends.

All of my high school friends have supported me over the years in all my endeavors, whether I was playing baseball, riffing on the saxophone, or appearing in shows and plays in high school.

I still see them at informal dinners at my house, or we all go out somewhere.

"We're all old North St. Louis folks from a typical blue-collar neighborhood. Most of our dads fought in World War II," remembers Jim Mathews, who played varsity baseball with me at Beaumont in our junior and senior years. After high school, where he was a football player, Jim went into the Army and had a 23-year career there. Later, he worked for Ameren UE. For all his achievements, he gave me some advice I'll never forget.

"Whatever you choose to do, do it with all your might to the point of being successful," he told me.

Cheerleader Buddy

Another one of my other good friends in high school was a cheerleader, Jo-Ann Cox (Bunton). Jan (my wife today) was already my girlfriend by then, but Jo-Ann and I had a lot of fun together, too. Jo-Ann remembers getting kicked out of the room during our radio class together because I was being flirtatious and said something off-color about her when I didn't realize the microphone was on.

"He was teacher's pet in that class," Jo-Ann recalls. Maybe that's why she got kicked out and I didn't! Anyway, we had a good laugh about that. Jo-Ann married her husband, Bob Bunton, right out of high school, and they went on to have seven beautiful kids.

"You always had personality-plus," she once told me.

Alan Wedemeyer, another close high school buddy, remembered that I always looked past the fact that he was – in his words – "a punk, who hung with the not-so-great kids." I always gave Alan a break because he tried hard, and he was a lot of fun.

"A lot of people don't realize that Hardy – we all called him that – was once one vote short of becoming class president. And in his adult life he was inducted into the Beaumont High School Hall of Fame," Alan said. "Bob was very intelligent, but he was not a nerd—he was a standout."

Alan went on to work in the building materials business, and I contacted him for advice when I was building my house in Chesterfield in 2000. He was a big help, and we became even closer friends.

CHAPTER TWO

The Big Sign-up

ON A CHILLY February day in 1959, my best friend, Buck, swung by my apartment at 3926 Kennerly Avenue in North St. Louis to drive me to Carbondale so I could claim my baseball scholarship and sign up for college and the team.

He was driving a garish green and yellow car that we loved. Friends cracked jokes, but we thought she was cool and named her The Poobah. Yeah, she was a little rough, but when Buck stepped on the gas pedal, the Poobah took off.

*I was on my way to Carbondale
with the thrill of excitement in my veins and
a little sadness in my heart
about leaving my family behind.*

Buck and his brother, Jack, had bought the car for $125 the year before. Buck never did pay his share of it, and to this day Jack still reminds me of that. Anyway, paid up or not, they shared the car, which had a big bench front seat, a makeshift backseat, and a gigantic trunk. We put a little soda case flat behind the front bench seat, so you could sit sideways in the back. That way you could fit three people in the car – and five in its gigantic trunk. Sometimes we'd cram the trunk with the only five guys who didn't care how the car looked, and we'd hit the drive-in.

But this February day, I jumped in the car, and we were off. I had on my favorite pair of jeans, a t-shirt, my tennis shoes and socks. That was it, despite temperatures in the 40s. I was on my way to Carbondale with the thrill of excitement in my veins, and a little sadness in my heart about leaving my family behind. This was my first time away from home.

And Then The Rains Came

Buck and I had just crossed the bridge going over the Mississippi River from St. Louis to Illinois when it began to rain – pouring rain. The Poobah's windshield wiper on the driver's side worked well, but there wasn't one on the shotgun side, which I pointed out to Buck. "You don't need a windshield wiper; you're not driving," Buck said as I shrank down in my seat. Five miles later, we came to a railroad track on Highway 13. Buck loved living on the edge, and stopped right on the railroad tracks. "Hey! Let's wait for a train." he said. "What? Are you crazy?" I shouted. "We could get killed." We looked left – no train. We looked right and – "Move it!" I hollered. There was a train bearing down on us.

Buck jammed the gear shift into first. We moved slowly and then jumped ahead off the tracks just as the train, with its whistle blowing, thundered right behind us, the train's vibration shaking the car.

"Buck! For crying out loud, what were you thinking?" I yelled.

Buck laughed. "Yeah, but we're having fun, aren't we?" I was deciding how to answer that when the tires squealed as Buck gunned the car, and we jerked forward. I settled into the seat as we sped ahead, the rain like bullets hammering the Poobah's hood. I guess this was fun – it was at least an adventure – and Buck was being a bit more careful, keeping two car lengths behind, but, still, we were going a daring 50 m.p.h., pushing the Poobah's limits.

Suddenly, the car in front of us swerved to the left to avoid hitting a dog sitting in the middle of the highway. Buck jammed on the brakes and turned the car to the left and with the back end coming forward, we slid and slid across the road, down an embankment, turned over once, maybe twice, and then came to a rolling stop upside-down. The dog, unhurt, stared at us in the window.

Big Damage

Buck's side of the car was completely smashed, so we had to climb out the window on my side, sliding out upside-down. When we got out, we stood in the rain looking at what was left of the Poobah. It was demolished. The dog, sensing trouble, ran off.

Finally a police car came. We went to the police station and filled out some paperwork. We said we'd come back for the car, but we never did; whether it was going to cost $20 or $100 to fix, we didn't have the money, so we left her – a green and yellow pile of rubble in a makeshift grave near the railroad tracks. And that was that.

The officer took us into the next town, Marissa, and we hitchhiked from one little Illinois town to the next: Columbia, Waterloo, Redbud, Evansville, Kaskaskia, and Chester, where the Menard state prison was. (I'd be inside that prison in the near future – but that's a different adventure.)

Once we were past Chester, where the highway ran close to the

Mississippi, we saw the big barges moving up and down the river. Then we were on to Murphysboro about 12 miles from Carbondale. Finally, four hours from the time we left my house, we were standing on Main Street in Carbondale – shell shocked from the wreckage we left behind but glad to be there.

Carbondale is on the edge of the beautiful Shawnee National Forest, in Jackson County, Illinois, and is at the junction of Illinois Route 33 and U.S. Route 51, 96 miles southeast of St. Louis. SIU-Carbondale, originally a teachers' and educational school, had an enrollment of 3,000 students when I was first there in 1959. By 2013, the enrollment had swelled to more than 25,900 students.

The Campus: The Lay of the Land — and 'UDs'

We walked through the town to the university and saw the Varsity Theater, Pizza Hut, University Drugs (dubbed "UDs" by the students), a couple of dorms, a clothing store called Goldstein's, and the university gymnasium – a large, brick building that housed the basketball court, the men's and women's locker rooms, the Athletics Department and the Intramurals Department where I was headed. I was to meet with Coach Martin – the one who had offered me a full working athletic scholarship. The working scholarship provided me with someplace to sleep (the dreary Dowdell Hall) and someplace to eat (Woody Hall where all the girls ate and lucky scholarship jocks like me got to join them). In exchange, I would work in the Intramural Department and be in charge of maintenance of the baseball field. SIU was on the quarter system, which included about 10 ½ weeks of studies, a week of finals, and then a 10-day break, unless you chose the summer term where school was out the middle of August and classes didn't start again until around the 20th of September.

The Illustrious Coach Martin

Coach Martin was about 6'2" and had played professional football with the Chicago Bears, and played in a national championship – he was a great athlete. He also coached one of the SIU-Carbondale basketball teams to another national championship. So this was a big-time coach, and I was nervous about meeting him again.

When he told me about the scholarship that previous summer, he'd also said he would help get me settled the day I signed up. So Buck and I went off in search of him. We walked into the athletics building, and there he was.

He got up, shook my hand and asked me how I was doing.

"Great, Coach," I said. "We had quite an experience coming up. We almost got run over by a train, nearly killed a dog, and totaled our car. But we made it." I introduced him to Buck. "This is my best friend, Buck. He's going to Kirksville on a football scholarship," (Kirksville is in Northeast Missouri).

*Phyllis took us
on a tour of the campus. She was so pretty
I checked her out
more often than the campus ....*

Coach smiled.

"Well son, we're really busy right now. This young lady here, Phyllis, is going to take you around to show you the campus and get you through the preliminary sign-up for school and classes. Then we'll see you at baseball practice in two weeks."

That was February 10, 1959. SIU was to have its spring break around March 15th. I was to come back to campus March 1st and stay with Coach Martin and his wife, Elise, at their home until the baseball team's spring trip, which I hoped to make. Around the very end of March when classes were to start, I would move into my new surroundings on campus. Little did I know how the next four years would go living at run-down Dowdell Halls.

Phyllis, who was remarkably pretty, took us on a tour of the campus. She was so pretty I checked her out more often than the campus, but I did see a few things. First, right outside the gymnasium, was a little fountain with a statue of a boy and girl holding an umbrella. Phyllis told us that this was the good luck spot on campus, and students made wishes there and tossed pennies in the fountain. Things were going great for me so I skipped the penny thing, although I would return again and again to the statue.

House of Cards: Dowdell Halls

Next was Old Main, which was the original building on campus – three stories, all brick, and 20-foot high ceilings – a monster of a building with no air conditioning. I was sure it would be hot in there in the summer. We moved on to Morris Library, and just past it was the baseball field, fenceless with an all-dirt infield – down the right field line, you could hit a ball 500 feet, and it was still in the playing field. I ran out to shortstop, strolled over to second base, and jogged over to third base. Those were my positions. That's where I was hoping to play first string, one position at a time.

Thompson Point was the biggest
and one of the nicest dormitories on campus.
Sadly, it was not mine.

We walked on and, in the center of the campus, we saw Thompson Woods, four square miles of spectacular forest and beautiful walking trails. The Thompson Family donated the land to the university with the stipulation that the land would have to stay as woods forever.

We walked the trails for awhile. The woods opened up on the other side to an on-campus beach and lake, which, though lovely, looked a little forbidding in February. We went on to the campus dorms. Thompson Point Dormitory was the biggest and one of the nicest on campus. Sadly, it was not mine. My dormitory, in the decrepit Dowdell Halls, was across from the railroad tracks and the football field. It's long since been torn down, but Dowdell Halls was a cluster of old army barracks lined up, side-by-side, seven in a row, with one of the buildings perpendicular to the others. That was the Dowdell office, where there was a mail drop, a pool table, and a ping pong table. The dorms had beat-up furniture because for fun the guys would throw the furniture against the walls, which were paper thin. My good college friend, Mike Pratt, called Dowdell Halls "The Cardboard Jungle."

When we went around the campus, we saw the Thompson Point Dormitory housed in a big brick building with beautiful rooms. While that wasn't my dorm either, I really didn't need to live anywhere fancy.

Next, on to the Registrar's Building, where I signed up for all my classes – English 101, Algebra 101, Health 101, History 101, and a class that everyone at SIU had to take, Music Appreciation. I was a saxophone and clarinet player, and all-around musician so when I found out we'd be taking Music Appreciation for two of our four years, I was thrilled.

A First: UDs' Monster Hamburger

After signing up, we went back to the Intramural Office and found Coach again. He could tell we were starved. To our relief he said, "Let's go over to UDs and grab a hamburger."

University Drugs, or UDs, was right across the street from campus and was kind of an unofficial student center. It had a cafeteria and drug store that sold everything from toothpaste to clothing. They had great food; but most importantly they had the unique UDs' hamburger. It was flat, as big as a large plate, and the cooks baked their own flatbread buns. The hamburger was cut in four pieces. The burger was smothered with lettuce, pickles, onions, tomatoes, mayonnaise, mustard, ketchup, barbeque sauce, salt, and pepper. Buck and I each devoured two of them, along with French fries and two Cokes.

"So, how are you boys going to get home?" Coach asked.

"We're gonna hitchhike," I said.

"Well, I'll drive you to the edge of town, and you can head out from there," Coach said.

Then it was back through the same towns we went through on the way up, and with no near-disasters, the trip home seemed a lot faster. It was a long day, but a great day for me, despite of the near-miss with the train, the rain, the dog, and — what hurt the most — the loss of the Poobah.

Buck and I spent the next couple of weeks working out at The YMCA across the street from Sportsman's Park, where the St. Louis Baseball Cardinals played. It was just the place for me to get into shape to play baseball and for Buck to get ready to play spring football at Kirksville. You name it, we did it – ran track, swam, lifted weights, played catch with baseballs and footballs, did sprints, push-ups, sit-ups, and jumping jacks. Finally both of us were ready for our first year of college.

CHAPTER THREE

Leaving Home

The thing was, my dad didn't know
how to get to Carbondale – he didn't even know how to read.

ON THE LAST day of February, we all piled in our family car, a 1940, two-door, black Plymouth with brown seats. Dad drove, and Tom and I sat in the back. Mom sat in the front with dad, and we were ready to go – except my dad didn't know exactly how to get to Carbondale. The only route my dad had traveled was from St. Louis to Little Rock, Arkansas, and back. He had a third-grade education and – I didn't find out till he died – he couldn't read.

Hard-Working, But Poor

My parents, Ann Marie and Hubert Columbus Hardcastle, were among the hard-working poor in St. Louis. As mentioned, we lived in a small apartment. My mother had a night job at a company called Amertorp, on Goodfellow Boulevard in St. Louis, a company that made torpedo parts during World War II. She later worked at St. Louis Screw and Bolt Co., which is still in business and now based in Madison, Illinois. Then she worked at Century Electric Co., a motor maker now operating as Magnetek Century Electric, Inc. in St. Louis.

We didn't see too much of Mom during the week, and I rarely saw Dad except at 6:00 a.m., when he'd take me to school (it wouldn't be open yet, but I'd sneak in, steal a softball and bat, go down to the bathroom, which was monstrous, and hit softballs against the wall for the two hours before school started).

The Original Krispy Kreme

I didn't see my dad much either because he worked 18 hours a day at his restaurant, which was on Ewing at Laclede Avenues, near Market Street in St. Louis. They moved in there in about 1938. But before that, he and my uncle owned a doughnut shop. They called it Krispy Kreme Doughnuts – spelled the same way it's spelled today.

One day, a guy came in and offered them $100 to buy the name and the recipe, and they sold both to him. I've got a picture of it. I'm sure my father's store was the original Krispy Kreme. Now they are everywhere.

'New' Victorian Digs — and Saying Goodbye

My dad eventually found his way to Carbondale despite his shaky directions and the emotional tension in the car. My excitement, and that of my family's, was tempered by our upcoming separation. When we pulled into Coach's driveway, he and his wife were waiting for us. Mrs. Martin led me into an old-fashioned room with a bed that seemed like it was five feet off the floor. It was an old, Victorian-style bed with high legs and two thick mattresses.

After a lunch of sandwiches and potato salad, it was time for Mom, Dad and Tom to go home.

I was now all alone, sitting on the ground next to Coach's pond,
scared and thinking,
'What have I done? Can I really go to college?
Can I make it on my own?'

I felt a pang of homesickness and hated to see them go. We kissed, hugged and said our good-byes with a lot of tears. I stood outside by myself and watched them drive away with my brother Tom waving at me out the back window. I could tell he missed me already. We had slept in the same bed all our entire lives.

After they left, I was now all alone, sitting on the ground next to Coach's pond, feeling scared and thinking "What have I done? Can I really go to college? Can I make it on my own?" The car was gone, the sun was down, the sky was black, and I was still sitting on the ground next to the pond when Coach shouted, "Hardy, it's about time to go to bed!"

I didn't fall asleep for quite a while. I could still see my brother Tom waving at me out the back window of the car. I laid awake for several hours, not only feeling homesick, but with those big questions looming.

First Day: Ugh! Oatmeal

The next morning we had oatmeal, which I hated. For as long as I can remember my dad made oatmeal for breakfast every day of my life. No eggs. No bacon. No cereal. Nothing but plain oatmeal and a glass of milk. This morning, Mrs. Martin put sugar and cinnamon on my oatmeal, and it tasted a little better. But it was still oatmeal.

I shoved it down fast, and then we were off to SIU! It was March 1st. I had graduated mid-term from high school at the end of January, 1959; the third quarter of SIU didn't start until April 1st. That was right when the baseball season started, but baseball practice had already been going on for about two months.

In Carbondale, you had to play in the gym on the basketball court during January and February. This was my first day of practice, but everybody else going out for the team had been practicing Monday through Friday for those first two months, so I had some catching up to do.

CHAPTER FOUR

Practice

'Well, if you are going to play,
you are going to have to chew.'

MY FIRST DAY of practice lasted seven minutes. Seriously. And it was all due to a run-in with some conniving players and my gullible acceptance of a jaw-full of chewing tobacco.

That day started out on rocky footing in the first place, what with the oatmeal I detested, and then my first encounter with a nasty old man named Grimes, who was in charge of handing out towels and workout clothes. I found the old man in a screened-in area inside the locker room. "Excuse me; are you Mr. Grimes?" I asked politely.

"So what if I am?" he said with a sneer.

"Well, Coach Martin told me I was supposed to see Mr. Grimes and get a roll," I said.

So, what kind of roll?" he asked gruffly.

"I don't know, sir," I said, my face reddening.

"Oh! So, you're a *baseball* player?" He sounded sarcastic.

"Yes, sir."

'Let's see . . . what's your name?"

"Hardy. H-A-R-D-Y."

"Hardy. . . Hardy. . . Bob Hardy. That's you?"

"Yes sir."

He threw a rolled up towel at me.

"Now, for you to get another roll, you've got to turn that one in exactly as I have given it to you. Everything that is part of that roll comes back, and then you'll get a new one. If you don't turn it all back in, you are not going to get another one. Got that?"

I bristled at his ounce of power. But I nodded and went back and sat on the bench in front of a locker. "Jerk," I thought. I unrolled the towel and saw a pair of socks that had *SIU* on each sock, an athletic supporter, and a short-sleeved t-shirt that said *SIU Athletics Department*. I put everything on, including some shorts that were in my gym bag. I grabbed my spikes, glove, and cap... wait a minute. All I had was my high school cap. I hated the thought of having to go back to old Grimes, but I did, and he tossed my new cap to me. It was maroon and had *Salukis* written across the front. I was official.

Rookie

I put my spikes on outside, while I sat on a wall surrounding the fountain of the girl and boy under an umbrella. Water was spouting from the top of the umbrella. I said hello to them and told them they would be seeing a lot more of me. I turned and ran toward the field.

With my spikes, I ran on concrete, grass, bricks, on grass again, on gravel and onto the ball field. As I was looking over the infield, which was all dirt and no grass, two ballplayers came up to me and asked, "You the new guy?"

I nodded and they introduced themselves as Ken, who played third base, and J.W., the catcher.

J.W. spoke up. "Well, if you are going to play, you are going to have to chew. Can you chew?"

I said, "Can I chew? Chew what?"

"Tobacco—have you ever tried it?"

"No."

J.W pulled out a big red and white bag out of his back pocket. He said, "Well, here's some Beechnut Tobacco. Take a big hunk. Now, put it in your mouth and don't swallow it."

I could hardly talk or breathe with that foul wad in my mouth. I had never even smoked tobacco before.

"OK, now, one more thing. Don't spit it out. Don't swallow it and don't swallow the spit. Just keep it in your mouth. Now to make the team, you have to do 100 sit-ups before practice every day."

So, with my mouth full of tobacco, I started doing sit-ups there in left field. They began laughing. I had just finished the sit-ups when I started coughing. I had swallowed some of the tobacco. Then I started spitting. I was swallowing and spitting. I spit out all of it that was still in my mouth. It seemed like half of it was gone. I told J.W. and Ken, "Man, I can't hack this."

By this time, now *they* were choking — with laughter. "Just go onto the infield," J.W. said between chuckles. "We'll try it again tomorrow."

Tobacco Woes: Turning Green

I started running onto the infield, but immediately felt wobbly, dizzy and sick to my stomach. I didn't know what was wrong with me.

My stomach was burning. Halfway between left field and shortstop, I puked and heard J.W. and Ken laughing behind me.

The Coach came over to me and asked, "What's wrong, boy? You look green."

"Well, I was chewing some tobacco."

"You were chewing some tobacco? Do you chew tobacco?"

"No sir, but J.W. and Ken told me that to make the team, I'd have to chew and do sit-ups."

"They did, did they? Okay, I'll tell you what. You go back to the locker room and see Doc. He'll fix something up for you because you are not in any position to play ball today."

"But Coach, I wanna play."

"Hardy, get back to the locker room and see Doc."

'You don't look like a baseball
player right now,' Doc said.
'In fact, you don't look like
much of a player at all.'

CHAPTER FIVE

Doc and a Bunch of Nasty Wrestlers

DOC LOOKED ABOUT 45, older than everyone else except Coach Martin. He was trim, muscular and had a lot of red hair. I heard he once played Major League Baseball. When I first saw him, he was laughing and seemed to really be enjoying what he was doing, taping up calves and wrists and treating wounds with alcohol. He had a belt around his waist that held scissors, gauze, tape, band-aids, and other stuff. A bunch of guys were ahead of me, so I just got in line. The fellow in front of me, a big guy, asked, "What's wrong with you, kid?"

"Ah, I chewed some tobacco."

"Oooh, you better get in front of me. You look sick, like you're about ready to die."

I asked him what was wrong with him, and he told me he had dislocated his thumb. I looked at his monstrous hand — his fingers were pointing straight up and his thumb was pointing straight down.

"Doesn't that hurt?" I asked.

"Nah, happens all the time." His name was Marion Rushing, who later played football as a defensive half-back with the St. Louis Football Cardinals.

I moved ahead of the big guy, and the next guy in front of me waved me on to the front of the line. His name was Fred Orlefsky, who became an All-American gymnast.

I said to Doc, "I'm Hardy. I'm a baseball player."

"You don't look like a baseball player right now. In fact, you don't look like much of a player at all. Tell me what happened."

As I was telling him, everybody in the training room started laughing hysterically. Doc was even chuckling. He said, "Look, we're not laughing at you; we're laughing at what happened. You really got taken for a ride. They wanted you to swallow the tobacco, and whenever you swallow tobacco, you get sick."

"Well, I'm never chewing tobacco again."

He said, "Well Hardy, I don't think you'll get the Johnson and Johnson Award today, but you are close."

"The Johnson and Johnson Award?"

"Yeah, every day I hand out the Johnson and Johnson Award to the athlete who had the dumbest and worst thing happen. You are close, but no cigar for you today." I grimaced at the image of a cigar. More tobacco. Ugh.

"Well, I'd hate to see the person who wins it," I said.

'Get out of here or I'll break your neck!
Close the door!'
the wrestler screamed at me.

"That guy over there," Doc said and pointed to a big athlete I met coming into the training room. "He won it."

"What did he do?"

"He was wrestling and ran into the wall. He busted his head on a pipe and knocked the wall in. He scraped himself up a little bit, but he'll be fine."

The Tobacco-Chewer's Antidote

"I'll tell you what," Doc said. "Here, take a couple of aspirin and drink a whole bunch of water. Stay in here for a while." He gave me an ice bag for the back of my neck and told me to relax on one of the benches for an hour.

During the next hour I met all the athletes in the training room – wrestlers, gymnasts, football players, track and field players, and cross-country runners. I cringed, but they all had a good laugh at me. When I got up, I got dressed quickly and went outside, looked around and there was Coach, waiting in his car to drive us back to his house.

On the way back, I relaxed, closed my eyes and as I settled in for the ride, I thought about how strange the day had been. Feeling drowsy, I mentally retraced my steps after I left the field, sick as a dog, and tried to find Doc ....

On my way to see Doc in the training room, I ran into Mr. Grimes again. I didn't need any of his ribbing or foul humor, so I told him right away I was sick from swallowing tobacco. He said I looked like I had just died.

"Kid, you don't swallow tobacco," he added. You chew it."

"I know that now," I said, annoyed. "I didn't mean to swallow it, but J.W. and Ken had me doing sit-ups after I stuffed a big handful of tobacco into my mouth and started chewing," I said.

"Huh! So, the rookie was indoctrinated."

I didn't want to hear anymore, so I asked Grimes where Doc was.

Grimes nodded his head in the direction of the training room. "Doc's in there."

I could hear Grimes chuckle as I walked away.

There was no writing on the first door I came to, but I figured it must be the training room. I opened the door – and got hit in the face with steam. I felt sicker than ever, and I couldn't see. I was standing there with the door open, steam flying out of the room.

Wrestler-speak

"CLOSE THAT DAMN DOOR! GET OUT OF HERE! CAN'T YOU TELL WE'RE HAVING PRACTICE?"

I still couldn't see anybody. Finally, out of the depths of the steam came a wrestler wearing a rubber suit – pants and top – and ear guards. He was screaming at me.

"GET OUT OF HERE OR I'LL BREAK YOUR NECK! CLOSE THE DOOR!"

I could just start to see the outline of various bodies on wrestling mats. It looked like the wrestlers were also doing jumping jacks, push-ups, sit-ups, and rolling on the floor doing different wrestling moves. They must have been crazy – hot, burning up. The wrestler standing in front of me shouted once again, "GET OUT OF HERE!" He pushed me out, and slammed the door.

Feeling sicker, I kept going down the hall until I found the training room.

This guy must have weighed at least 350 pounds
and was the biggest, blackest man
I had ever seen.

I had a hard time taking it all in. The room was filled with padded benches, athletes, and apparatuses hanging from the ceiling. There was a guy climbing up to a homemade chin-up bar. He was hanging on what looked like sawed-off baseball bat handles, holding himself up with one handle while he put the other handle into the next hole up the rung. He would then shift his weight to the other handle, pull out the handle on the lower rung and move it to the next hole up the rung. He went up, down, sideways and at an angle. I couldn't believe he could do it. He was on the small side, but muscular. Then I noticed a huge guy, who had to be a football player or a wrestler. I found out later he was both. This guy must have weighed at least 350 pounds and was the biggest, blackest man I had ever seen. He was looking right at me, and when he spoke he had this funny high-pitched voice. I was trying to remember the sound of his voice when I blinked my eyes open, and we were back at Coach's house.

CHAPTER SIX

A Second Chance

THE NEXT DAY, I felt fine and knew where I was going, but first I had to deal with Grimes again. I went into the locker room and asked him for a roll, and he asked me my name again, as if he didn't know. "I'm Hardy. The one who got sick yesterday."

"Boy, a lot of the athletes got sick yesterday, but you were the only one who turned green," he said, throwing me a roll. I backed away from him before he could say another word, and put on my uniform.

Before I went out to the field, I went back to the training room. On my way, I noticed that big door. Could they still be in there? By now those guys would have lost all kinds of weight. So I turned the knob and opened it slowly. No steam hit me in the face so I figured no one was in there, but when I looked in there were two wrestlers on mats, one little guy, who weighed about 125 pounds, and one huge guy — the big athlete that was in the training room the day before who had pointed me toward Doc. I guess it was the coach that was yelling, "IZZY, STAY DOWN. STAY ON YOUR HANDS, ELBOWS AND KNEES. KEN, TAKE HIM DOWN."

I had no idea what was going on and didn't realize that their angry, red-nosed coach was looking at me and snarling. He pushed me out and slammed the door. I finally figured out that I'd better stay away from the wrestlers. They looked vicious (The only exception was a nice guy named Deek, a blind wrestler, whom I'd met one of the first days I was on campus. I helped him across an intersection by telling him there was a green light. He always remembered my voice. I still don't know how he managed to deal with the rest of those nasty wrestlers).

I left, and walked down toward the training room and looked in. Doc was busy at work taping up an athlete's ankles. It turned out to be the little guy, Fred, who was doing the chin-ups the day before. I walked over to Doc and said, "I'm Hardy. I just wanted to thank you for yesterday."

"Oh, how you feeling? You don't look green anymore," Doc said.

"No, you look pretty good in fact," Fred chimed in.

Back to The Infield: Let's Try This Again

I thanked them and went to my locker, grabbed my spikes, glove and hat and took off for the ball field. I put my spikes on while sitting on the edge of the fountain. I said hello again to the boy and girl under the umbrella at the fountain. For some reason, I thought they heard me. Then it was over the concrete, past Old Main, through the grass, over the bricks, past Morris Library, back on the grass, through the gravel, past the parking lot, through the outfield and onto the infield, which was further than I had gotten the day before.

Coach called us all together at the start of practice. He told us to warm up, stretch, touch our toes, and run five laps around the ball field. Then we all lined up: half along the first baseline between home plate and first base, and the other half on the baseline between third and second. We threw to a partner standing on the opposite side of the infield, warming up our arms. That way no one would get hit by a wild throw.

So, what's a Fungo? It's a skinny, weird-looking bat
that make it easier to hit ground balls
and pop-ups.

We threw the ball back and forth, trying to throw the ball to our partners, hitting them about chest-high on their catching side. The outfielders lined up in deep centerfield and threw to their throwing partners along the left-field line. They would play catch and then throw a much further distance than the infielders. That's because the outfielders had strong arms that could throw the ball between 200 to 300 feet or more. The infielders needed to throw the ball less than 120 feet, which they did – well, most of the time.

A-Bunting We Must Go

At batting practice, each of the players got five swings after making three bunts. Coach said bunting allowed us to move runners along to the next base, squeeze bunt them home, and possibly get a base hit. Bunting made me keep my eye on the ball, like bottle caps used to in the alleys of St. Louis. Coach said we wanted to watch the ball hit the bat, with our top hand sliding up the bat to cushion the blow.

The next player, who had been waiting in the on-deck circle, was hitting balls off a tee, just concentrating on swinging and hitting the ball right into a net. At the same time, the two assistant coaches were using the Fungo bats, hitting ground balls to the infielders, one hitting from the right side of the batting cage and one hitting from the left. The

33

Fungo hitters would alternate, hitting just after a batter would take one of his swings. This made everything move more quickly, wasting less time and achieving more during the practice.

So, what's a Fungo? It's a weird-looking bat. It's skinnier than a regular bat, long and narrow. It's easier to hit ground balls and pop-ups with a Fungo bat. It doesn't take as much energy or strength, but it takes a lot more timing to swing a Fungo bat and hit the ball.

From Outfield to Infield

After batting practice, Coach told everybody to go to their positions. He grabbed a Fungo bat. The catcher, J.W. – my nemesis from the day before – grabbed about eight balls and threw them in a bag. Coach yelled, "Nobody on base, everybody go to their positions when the ball is hit!" He hit a ball to the right-fielder. The second baseman went out to receive the relay, standing in a direct line between the right-fielder and second base. As the shortstop, I went to second base. The right-fielder threw the ball to the second baseman and the second baseman relayed the ball to me. Coach hit the ball to the left-fielder. So I went out to get the relay and then turned around and threw it to second base. Coach did the same thing to the center fielder, but the ball drifted over to the right side of the outfield, so the second baseman went out to receive the relay, and I went to second base. If the ball had gone to the left field side, then I would have caught the relay and thrown it to the second baseman.

"Okay, there's a man on first base!" Coach yelled, signaling us to pay attention. He hit hard ground balls to the outfielders. Depending on whether the ball was hit right to them or not, the players lined up exactly the same way. If the ball was hit directly to the right-fielder, the second baseman would go out; the shortstop would cover second. If it was hit to the left-fielder, the shortstop would go out to get the relay, and the second baseman would cover second base. When the ball was hit directly to the center fielder, the shortstop and the second baseman would let each other know which one was going out to receive the relay (depending on whether the ball was to the right or left side), and who was going to cover second base.

Then we had infield practice. Coach and J.W. moved back behind home plate. Coach would hit a ground ball to each of us at third, short, second, and first. We would simply catch the ball and throw it to first base, as if we were throwing someone out. The first baseman would catch his ground ball, run to first, and step on the bag for the out. Then Coach would say, "Man on first base." He'd hit the ball the same way to each of us, but we would try for a double play.

Then it was my turn. Coach hit a ball to me at shortstop, pretty close to second base. Our second baseman, Itch, came over to cover second base. I whirled and threw it – almost through him. He yelled out, "Wait a minute! Wait a minute, Hardy! What are you trying to do, kill me? Look, when you are that close, it's like giving candy to a baby. Just rotate towards me and flip the ball underhanded so I can see it all the way into my glove. Then I can relay it to first base."

"Sorry Itch. I didn't mean to try to kill ya!"

Coach hit another ground ball to me. The ball was between second base and shortstop. I grabbed the ball, rotated toward Itch, then showed him the ball as he was coming toward second base, and I flipped it to him underhanded. He caught it, pivoted and threw to first. He looked at me.

"Hardy, that's a lot better. See? Just like giving candy to a baby."

Years later, in 1970, Itch would take the job Coach Martin had and become head baseball coach at SIU-Carbondale. After that, he became head baseball coach at the University of Illinois at Champaign. He retired in 2005.

As for my baseball abilities, Itch recently acknowledged that by college, I had come a long way from my rookie year.

"I remember how hard Hardy worked, that he was a very aggressive ballplayer, and a wonderful guy to play with. He kept everyone's spirits up by being a great leader and doing a lot of great hitting," he said.

A Gymnast Performs a Mystical Miracle

After practice one day, I walked out to the Intramural Office. Coach was having a meeting and told me to come back in 10 minutes. I started to walk through the hall to go outside when I noticed the wrestlers running the stairs. They said Coach told them they had to run up and down the stairs 50 times a day after practice. I was impressed!

"What's upstairs?" I asked one of the wrestlers, and he said the basketball court, gymnasium, and offices.

I was eligible for the southern trip,
but Coach had to decide
if I was a good enough player to go.

I waited until the wrestlers were finished, and I walked up the stairs to the gym where the only light that came through the windows was on the opposite side of the gym floor. I noticed two gymnasts talking on the opposite side of the court. The slender fellow, whom I had met in Doc's training room, went over to the straps that were hanging down with wooden-circled handles at the end – the rings. They hung down

36

from the ceiling to about seven feet off the floor. His partner helped him jump up, and he curled his right hand around the right ring and his left hand around the left ring. His partner held him steady as he hung straight down.

Then the partner walked away and the gymnast remained in place. Astonishing! I had never seen anything like this before. The gymnast holding onto the rings brought himself straight up, with his legs extended straight out in front of him, holding himself perfectly upright from the waist. He then lowered his legs and slowly let his muscular arms go out sideways, right arm to the right side, left arm to the left side, until his straightened arms were holding him steady. Then he pulled his arms back in and let himself hang straight down and dropped to the floor.

The light coming in from the windows made it look like a mystical miracle. How did he do that?

CHAPTER SEVEN

Rookie: The Spring Baseball Trip

EVERY YEAR, SIU-CARBONDALE baseball players took a spring trip. Sometimes the team would go out West and play Arizona State, the University of Arizona, or other schools in Arizona. Sometimes they'd take a southern trip into Louisiana, Alabama, Arkansas, or Mississippi. This year the spring trip was to Louisiana. We were going to leave March 18th, at the end of the next week. Coach said he would post a list of all the players who were chosen to go on the bulletin board outside the Intramural's room on March 16th. Even though I hadn't started my classes yet, I was enrolled and that allowed me to be eligible for the southern trip, but Coach had to decide if I was good enough to make the trip. Making the southern trip would mean I was really part of the team.

The next few days passed quickly, as I helped Coach with his outline for his classes; I also bailed hay, and dug fence posts at his house. On March 16th we had practice as usual. After practice, Coach called us all together and said, "Now boys, I'm going to post who's going to make the southern trip. We will leave in two days, on the 18th. So, if you are going on the trip, get your gear ready and meet here at 6:00 a.m. that day. For you boys who don't make the southern trip, everybody going out for the team right now is still on the team, so I expect you to stay in shape while we are gone for the next ten days and be here for practice the first day we get back."

The 17th Name on the List

I was nervous. I knew I was the only rookie who hadn't yet started college, but I still hoped I could go on the trip.

On the way back to the locker room, I stopped off at the fountain, and as I was taking off my spikes, I told the boy and girl under the umbrella, "Well, here we go. In a little while, I will find out if I'd made the southern trip. If not, I still have a chance to make the team. Look at you. Both of you at least have an umbrella. It's just me now. I don't have any cover. It's whatever I've done, whatever I've shown Coach. Well, hold yourselves close, say a prayer for me, and I'll let you know what the results are when I come out."

I headed back to the locker room and cleaned up. By that time, everybody had already left the room and had crowded outside the In-tramural's Office. Some were yelling; some were screaming. I walked through the locker room door. I saw them jumping and hollering, but all I was doing was looking at the bulletin board. Eighteen players were going. I stared at the list for a long time until I got to the 17th name. It was bigger than any letters I had ever seen – BOB HARDY. I was as excited as I'd been in a long time. I ran out. As I passed the fountain, I cheered, "Hey guys, I made it! I made it! Thanks! I made it! You helped. Thanks!"

As Coach and I walked out to the car, I thanked him and told him how excited I was.

He said, "Well, you deserve it. Just show me you can play ball and do well in school at the same time."

"Yes, sir. I will."

I looked at my Number 19
in big maroon numbers.
How cool was that?
It knocked me out, and I jumped up in the air.

When we got home, Coach's wife gave me a big hug. I called my mom and dad and told them about the trip. They sounded as excited as I was. Everything was great! I had never been so happy. I couldn't wait.

The Magic Number: 19

The next day, I went out to the ball field making sure all the equipment was ready, and I loaded the U-Haul that was pulled behind Coach's car until all our balls, bats and equipment were stacked inside. I killed some time watching the wrestlers and gymnasts practice in the gym. The next thing I knew it was 2 p.m., the time Coach said to pick up our travel gear.

I went into the locker room and saw a smiling Mr. Grimes. "I'm really happy you made the team and the spring trip," Mr. Grimes said, sounding so sincere I was almost touched. He gave me a large travel bag that had "Southern Illinois University Baseball" written across the bottom. I went to the far end of the locker room so I could be by myself. I slowly unzipped the bag and found three pairs of regular socks and two pairs of sanitary socks, the ones baseball players wear over the regular

41

socks, which rise up to the thigh. I also found maroon-colored stirrup socks, and my new maroon hat with SIU lettered in the front. I put it on and it fit perfectly. Then I found a long, maroon-sleeved, off-white sweatshirt that I would wear under my uniform jersey. The pants were off-white with a maroon stripe down each side. I pulled out my jersey with the letters S O U T H E R N on the front. I looked at my number: 19, written in big maroon numbers on the back. How cool was that? It knocked me out, and I jumped up in the air. I was almost embarrassed at how happy I was. I put the uniform on, all of it held together by my thick belt, and I walked to a full-size mirror and stared. There I was. Hardy. I made the team, I made the trip, and I was ready to go.

Southward, Ya'll – to Baton Rouge and Beyond!

We were going to Louisiana State University in Baton Rouge, to play a series of three games against them. Then we were going to several other colleges in Louisiana to play ball there. Traveling was sort of new to me. Except for the team trip to New York City in high school, I'd never been further away than Little Rock, Arkansas, near where my grandparents lived, in a little town called Jacksonville.

Coach and I were up at 3:30 a.m. on March 19th, and we finished packing the U-Haul that was to be pulled behind the lead car he was going to drive. We headed to the campus.

We had five cars for the 18 ballplayers, Coach, and his assistant. (The cars we drove on the southern trip were made by Checker Motors. Checker Cabs were the most famous taxis in the United States at the time. They were green and cream-colored, roomy and rugged, with a lot of space between the front seat and the back seat. Coach assigned each ballplayer to a car, three to five of us to a car. The caravan of cars finally took off. I was in the fourth car with Itch (the second baseman) at the wheel, Jerry (the other shortstop), Mike (the second-string third baseman) and Monty (another infielder). When we got tired along the way, one of us would lie on the floor between the front and back seats. The other two in the back seat would take the left and right sides. One of us would stick our legs up on the rear window, and the other would bend our legs across the back seat.

I felt like I was in a different country.
It was still cold in Carbondale, but now,
just several hours south of Illinois,
the sun was shining, and it was warmer.

Coach told us we should talk a lot in the car about how we were going to play left-handed hitters and right-handed hitters, decide who was going to cover second base on a steal, and anything else we could think of. We came up with a terrific way for the shortstop and second baseman to let the other player know who was going to cover second base on a steal. If the batter was left-handed, then the shortstop (me) would move more towards second base. For a right-handed hitter, I'd move a little further away from second base. With a left-handed batter, I'd move over closer to second base and look at Itch, who would put his glove up to his face so no one on the opposing team's bench could see his face. Then, Itch, who was captain of the infield, would give me a signal, "open mouth," which meant I would cover the base. A "closed mouth" meant Itch would cover. He called all the plays which made me feel really good. I certainly didn't want to make a rookie mistake and have the whole team jump on me.

43

We also discussed who would cover first base on a bunt and how important it was if a man was on first base for the third baseman to go back to third base quickly after catching a bunt down the third base line to throw the ball to first base. If the third baseman didn't get back to third base quickly after making the throw, the runner from first base, who would be heading to second base, might decide to go to third base. If no one was at third base, the runner could just coast in. We worked on these types of plays a lot.

The Music Men

We also got around to the subject of music. Mike played the trumpet. I played the sax and clarinet, and Jerry played drums. I said, "Let's have a jam session." The classic "St. Louis Blues" was playing on the radio, so each of us acted like we had our instrument with us and started playing along with the song. Jerry was be-bopping on the drums. Itch was banging the steering wheel, giving it all he had. The trumpet was going "Ba bum, Ba ba, Ba bum, Ba ba," and I was playing the clarinet "Ba da da doobie doobie doobie do bop." We had our own infield travel band going and we were sure we had more fun in our car than the other players had in theirs.

Eat Fast and Don't Fall Down!

When we would go through a town, each car would flash its lights to make sure we followed each other closely. We had been on the road for about six hours when Itch said it was about time to pull over for lunch. "Okay now, here's the deal Hardy," he said. "We have to let you know about Coach's eating habits."

I waved them off. "I've eaten with Coach now for the last two-and-a-half weeks."

"No. You've eaten with Coach at home. You haven't eaten with him on the road," Jerry said. "He likes to chow down first and then gives you no time to eat. What you have to do is get in front of Coach before he gets in line to order. Don't let Coach order before you. We all try to make sure Coach is the last to order. The whole team needs to order first."

My SIU buddy, Mike Pratt, said he would grab some fried chicken off his plate and take it with him. "You had to if Coach was first in line," he remembered.

And, Yep, First in Line

Coach parked the car quickly at a diner and walked inside.

"That's bad news. He'll be the first one to order," Itch said. Not fully realizing the gravity of the situation I said, "Wait a minute! I left my wallet in the car." As I started walking back with my wallet, Itch yelled out as he was going into the diner, "You don't need it. Coach pays for it." So I went back to the car, put my wallet back on the rear seat, locked the car and went in. Everybody was standing in line. Coach was first in line, pulling his food tray along and filling it with food as he worked his way towards the register. I was last. I got my food, and as I was about to step away from the checkout line, Coach said, "Okay, boys! Let's go!" I looked at Itch, and he said, "Let's go!" I grabbed a paper plate, put my lunch on it, and went rushing out, only to stumble when my shoe caught a raised area in the floor at the door entrance. I hit the ground. The open-faced roast beef sandwich flew everywhere. I didn't have time to pick it up; I just rolled over and ran as if I was headed to home plate.

The guys said, "Get in! Get in quick!" Coach had already taken off. The second car was gone and so was the third. I jumped in the fourth car, and Itch looked at me and said, "See, Rookie, we told you. You've gotta eat quick, and don't be the last in line."

Later, with my stomach growling, I looked out the window and noticed Spanish moss, exotic and beautiful, growing on the trees. I felt like I was in a different country. It was still cold in Carbondale, but now just several hours south of Illinois, the sun was shining, and it was warmer.

We stopped one more time to eat supper. I was hungry and made sure I was first in line, and the rest of the team made sure Coach was last. I thought I had plenty of time, but just in case, I ordered soup and milk, which I downed right away, and a ham and cheese sandwich. I saw that Coach was still eating, so I took about two bites of my sandwich, but he got up to leave. "Okay boys, let's go." I wrapped the rest of my sandwich in a napkin. This time I didn't trip.

After dinner, *"Going to New Orleans"* was playing on the radio. We started our Dixieland band and just went crazy, playing and singing: *"Going to New Orleans* – "Ba bum, Ba ba, Ba bum, Ba ba."

> *I pulled a rookie mistake in our first game on the road.*
> *Without getting a signal from Coach,*
> *I got so excited, I tried to steal third base.*
> *I was out before I even started to slide.*

At 10:30 p.m., we pulled into LSU. We were staying on campus in the men's locker room where all visiting teams stayed. It was really cool, my first night on the road with the team.

We were all sound asleep on cots in the cavernous locker room when, promptly at 6 a.m., Coach yelled out, "Okay, boys. Let's get up and get ready for practice." We got up and put on our uniforms. The baseball field was out one door, but I noticed a big opening through another door. I went through it, and it turned out to be the opening the football teams pass through to get onto the impressive football field. I turned around to walk back in and saw writing on the wall above me. It was a line I had never seen before: "When the going gets tough, the tough get going."

"Yeah," I thought. "I'm ready."

Coach put me in to bat in the seventh inning. With a man on first base, I hit a double, bringing the man on first in. He ran all the way around the bases, scored, and I was on second base. Then I pulled a rookie mistake. Without getting a signal from Coach, who was standing in the third base coaching area, I got so excited, I tried to steal third base. I was out before I even started to slide. That was the third out of the inning. Coach just looked at me like, "What are you doing?" but he didn't say a word.

I ran to get my glove and started to go to shortstop, but Jerry was there. I turned around to look at Coach, and he said, "You're the right-fielder." I had never played right field before, but at least I was playing. I went out to right field. No one hit to me in the seventh or eighth inning. I liked it that way. We were winning 4-2. At the bottom of the ninth inning, they got their first two men on base, and then we walked the third man. They had bases loaded with nobody out.

Blinded by the Light

In right field I could see the sun setting behind the batter, but I couldn't really see him. I was standing there wondering, "What am I doing out here?" and the next thing I knew, the batter hit a fly ball that looked like it was coming to me. I staggered, trying to see the ball. I put my glove up. I thought I had it! Nope. I cried out, "I can't see it! I can't see it." I heard our center fielder running real hard, shouting, "I GOT IT! I GOT IT!" He ran right in front of me, grabbed the ball and threw home. The runner went back to third base. And did I feel stupid!

We were still winning, 4-2, and we had one out, but they had loaded the bases. The next guy came up and hit another fly ball right to me, but this time, I saw it all the way.

"I've got it! I've got it!" I yelled. I caught the ball. The runner on third base tagged. I threw the ball to home plate, and with one bounce, J.W. caught the ball. The runner slid into home. J.W. tagged him out for the third out to end the game. We won 4–2.

Coach never said anything to me about missing that ball or stealing third base. In fact, Coach never said anything to me at all except, "I want you to play well, to play smart, follow the signals, and do well in school."

I promised him I would. And from then on, I was the starting shortstop. I don't know how that worked out, but it did. I didn't ask any questions; I just played shortstop with all the enthusiasm I could gather.

'It's Alive!'

One night in Louisiana, we went out to dinner at a place called "The Bayou." The restaurant's waiters and waitresses were telling us to order the soft-shelled crab, shrimp, mussels, and snails – their specialties. This was pretty exotic food for a kid overfed on oatmeal, but I wouldn't have missed it. I think the food was new to my teammates too. When Itch went to the bathroom, the assistant coach went into the kitchen and asked for a live crab on a plate. By the time he came back out, we had already been served. The assistant coach flipped the little crab on the top of Itch's plate of food. We all started eating, stifling laughs, and waited for Itch to come back.

When he returned, he sat down on his bench, took his knife and fork, looked at his plate, and said he was game to try it. He took his fork and stuck it in the top of the crab not knowing it was alive.

The crab raised its legs. Itch screamed, fell over backwards off the bench and found himself staring straight into the kitchen. He yelled, "They served me a live crab, and now there's an alligator in the kitchen! It's alive!" he screamed. We all got up to see. Yep, an alligator was on the floor. It yawned lazily and gave us the eye. The waitresses told us it was their pet. We finished dinner and skedaddled out of there.

A Wild Ride with a Beautiful Stranger

After our first week we had done real well, winning six out of eight games, and now we were pulling into Hammond and Louisiana's Strawberry Stadium. Again we were staying in the men's field house, where all visiting players stayed. After the car ride I felt like taking a walk.

I almost bumped into her, and when I stepped back, she took my breath away. Dressed in a tight orange skirt with a slit on one side, she also had on a white blouse with an open neckline. She had the greenest eyes, and her light brown hair was cut in a pageboy.

"Hey! Where ya'll going in such a hurry?" she asked.

"Well, I really don't know where I'm going — I'm just walking around the campus."

"You don't sound like you're from around here."

"Well, I'm not. I'm just here for a baseball game against the Lions tomorrow. And by the way, your accent doesn't sound familiar to me either."

49

"Look Yankee, you're in the South now. This is how all of us sound, ya hear?"

She asked where I was from, and I explained that I was from St. Louis, and that I was traveling with the baseball team from SIU-Carbondale.

I stuck out my hand. "My name's Bob, but everybody calls me Hardy. What's yours?"

She blushed a bit and shook my hand. "Ashley. You can call me Miss Ashley." She asked if I'd like to take a ride, and I said, "Sure, y'all."

We walked through campus and jumped into a brand new, black Chevy Impala.

We drove out of town. It was getting dark, but we kept driving along the bayous. When we got to a restaurant/bar, she stopped, and we went inside. She said hello to a couple of people and ordered a beer. I ordered a Coke. We talked about the campus, the baseball team and what position I played. We were having a good time just talking and relaxing. Then, after a while, she said, "Well, I guess I'd better get you back to the ball field. It wouldn't look good for me to keep an opposing team's player out real late at night so he couldn't play well the next day."

So we went back to the car and took off. Just a little while later, she pulled over to the side of the road. Then she pulled off a little bit further.

"Well Yankee, what do you think about our town?" she asked.

"Well," I said, "What I've seen looks real good."

She leaned over and gave me a kiss on the lips. So I kissed her back. Pretty soon, we were making out furiously. After a few minutes, my hands started roving. But she was having none of that. "Now, Yankee, we don't want any Northern aggression from a Yankee down here, do we?" she asked.

Breathing deeply I said, "Well, I guess not."

'Stay North of My Shoulders, Yankee'

She took my hands and raised them to her shoulders, patted them down and said, "Let's keep kissing, but why don't you keep your hands above the Mason Dixon line, above my shoulders. You stay north of that and we'll have no problems." So, being the good Yankee that I was, I continued to just kiss her for a very long time.

I got back into the dorm just before curfew which was 10:00 p.m. I was rooming with Itch and Jerry. They asked, "Where were you?"

"Well, I took a long walk," I said.

"We were looking for you but couldn't find you. You must have taken a real long walk."

"Yeah, and it was a good one," I said. "I met this gorgeous girl with green eyes and a Southern accent who charmed the pants off me. Well, almost. We went to a bar and then we parked for awhile."

I yawned. "Well, time to hit the bunk," I said walking off, leaving Itch and Jerry in the dust, their jaws dropped to the ground.

A bunch of heads stuck out
of the car windows. They started whistling and
cat-calling, and mocking Miss Ashley.

Southern Louisiana State had a great ball field with beautiful grass on the infield and the outfield completely fenced in. You had to give the ball a pretty good poke to get it out of their ballpark. We won 7-3. I went three for four. There was a big crowd at the game. I didn't know if Miss Ashley, the Southern belle I had met the night before was at the game, but there was a lot of cheering from a bunch of gals in one section of the stands.

When the game was over, Coach, as usual, was anxious to get on the road. We were headed back to Carbondale. We showered and dressed quickly, got in our cars, and had just started to take off when four girls, one of them my Southern belle, Miss Ashley, walked up to the lead car and started talking to Coach. He pointed them in the direction of the car I was in, and the girls, each carrying two big brown bags, headed our way.

"What the ... ?" Itch said.

The Strawberry Queen

"Oh, my God! – that's the girl from last night!" I said, embarrassment creeping up my neck.

"Oh! Okay," Itch said. "We have this whole ride back to Carbondale to get the goods on what happened last night, but what have they got?" Miss Ashley walked up to the car and said to me, "Yankee, ya'll didn't think you were gonna git outta town without some of our goodies now, did ya?"

A bunch of heads stuck out of the windows of the other cars. They started whistling, cat-calling, and mocking Miss Ashley. "Hey Yankee!" they shouted. "Hardy, you didn't think ya'll were gonna git outta here without any goodies, did ya?" The guys were yelling, "Yeah, man. How about those goodies?" By this time, I was beet-red, but I stepped out of the car to be polite. She smiled and said, "We just brought ya'll strawberries, 40 quarts – some for everybody."

"Ah, that's great! Thank you so much!" I said, thankful that she was just giving us strawberries – I didn't know what else she might be giving us but, somehow, I felt relieved. We divided the strawberries up among all of the cars, as the yelling and cat-calling continued. "Thanks for your goodies, girls," the guys shouted. Then, right in front of every-body, Miss Ashley leaned in towards me. I leaned towards her and gave her a kiss on the cheek. She whispered in my ear, "Yankee, you did a lot better than that last night." She then stepped in closer to me, gave me a big hug, and we kissed. The fellows whistled and yelled. "Go for it, Hardy Boy," one hollered. The other girls cheered. I said good-bye and thanked Miss Ashley.

The cars pulled out. The girls all waved. Miss Ashley blew me a kiss, and we were on our way – so long to my first spring baseball trip. So long to the Spanish moss trees, the Bengal tigers, the right field, and so long to Miss Ashley. I wondered if I would ever see her again.

CHAPTER EIGHT

House of Cards

THAT NIGHT, AFTER we arrived back in Salukiville (a.k.a. Carbondale), we turned in our gear, and I went to find 600 Dowdell Halls where I was going to live the first quarter. Coach said I would have a roommate and reminded me that my meals and room and board would be paid by with my working scholarship. I would eat all of my meals at Woody Hall, an all-girls dorm. That sounded promising.

I headed toward Dowdell Halls to find my room, which was 624, at the end of the hall.

In the hallway, I noticed that about every four steps there was a door on each side with cardboard-like walls between each door. The walls had patched up holes, and all of the walls were torn up in some way – no wallpaper and nothing was painted. It was kind of like a cardboard building. Halfway down, there was an open door and inside the door I saw eight sinks with mirrors above each sink, and a long wall with eight showers.

I reached the end of the hall and knocked on room 624. My roommate-to-be opened the door.

"Hey man! Whatcha want?" he asked.

"I'm Bob. I'm assigned to this room."

"I'm Jerry. Come on in!"

He told me this was his first shot at going to college and to help meet expenses, he was working at UDs. He already had the bottom bunk, so I took the top. We both had a closet which held all my clothes – four shirts, two pairs of khaki pants, one pair of blue jeans, one pair of tennis shoes, one pair of dress shoes, my underwear and my gym bag (with weights in it). That was it.

The music teacher played a lot of jazz,
and we got to hear and see musicians like
J.J. Johnson, the famous trombonist,
and Dave Brubeck on the piano.

I climbed up on the top bunk and was asleep in seconds.

All That Jazz

The next day I got up early, looking forward to seeing the lovely Phyllis, who was going to help me time my classes so I could fit in baseball practice and the games. I scheduled English 101, Social Studies 101, P.E. 101, Early American Literature 102, Math 101, and Music Appreciation. I also had to sign up for ROTC (Reserved Officer Training Core) which was a requirement in those days. Everything had to be scheduled so that I'd have 3 p.m. to 6 p.m. free every day for baseball practice and games. In addition to baseball, I was really looking forward to Music Appreciation. It turned out to be better than I thought because the teacher played a lot of jazz, and we got to hear and see musicians like J.J. Johnson, the famous trombonist, and Dave Brubeck on the piano.

The music, the other classes, baseball, and my work caring for the field and the equipment reminded me how cool it was to do all that while I was getting a full scholarship.

The next day was the first day of classes. The alarm went off at 7 a.m. I got up, went to shave, brush my teeth and shower, but was confronted with about 20 guys scrambling to get in eight shower stalls and use eight sinks. They were shaving, washing, brushing, yelling, screaming, singing, dancing, showering and throwing what they called, "Jellyfish Jazz" over all the rookies. I managed to dodge the "Jellyfish Jazz," which was a good thing once I found out what it was.

There were four football players, Vic, Pod, Jim and Pete, who, every time they took a shower, would lather themselves up and then squeeze the soap off from around their private parts and flip it on the rookies or whoever was shaving.

They'd say, "Hey Boys! Here's some 'Jellyfish Jazz.'"

The victims yelled back, and threw water, toothpaste or whatever at them, but they'd been had. The four football players just loved splattering anyone with their "jazz," but rookies were their favorite targets. Every morning it was the same deal. You'd try to sneak in either before they got into the shower or after they were out.

Look Out! An All-Jock Dorm

Everybody in our dorm, except for three students, was an athlete at SIU – football, basketball, gymnastics, tennis, track, baseball, cross-country, and wrestling. We had guys who were 6'8" who weighed over 350 pounds. One fellow on the wrestling team was 5'2" and weighed 120 pounds. So in addition to the "Jellyfish Jazz," routine, you can imagine the scene in the shower room.

But not all the guys on campus were like the four football players. I soon met a lot of nice guys, too – Jim, Pete, Don, and a bunch more. I also met our Resident Counselor Bill who lived in the first room at the front of the hall. He was yelling at everybody that there was going to be a mandatory meeting that night at 6 p.m. to go over the rules for living in the dorm.

'Don't ask for any special privileges
like missing class
for a sporting event.'

I dressed quickly, went to my first class, English, and walked right into a big problem.

"I want you to know a few things," the instructor said. "First, you can't miss a class." Oh great, I thought. I was going to be playing baseball and missing a lot of classes. We had ballgames every Tuesday, Friday and Saturday.

"Is anybody in here on any of the sports teams?" he asked. I raised my hand, as did another fellow. The instructor's eyes pierced into us. "Don't ask for any special privileges like missing class for a sporting event," he said. "In fact, you might want to assign yourself to another English class, as athletes don't do real well in my class." That woke me up. I would have to discuss this with Coach.

At 2 p.m., I didn't have any more classes that day, only baseball practice. I went to the locker room, nodding to Grimes as I picked up my roll. I dressed in my baseball gear, then grabbed my hat and spikes and ran out the door. I put my spikes on outside sitting on the edge of the fountain, then ran across campus, around Shryock Auditorium, through the parking lot, and onto left field.

When I looked around, nobody was there. I couldn't understand it. It was 2:20 p.m. Where was everybody? I just started running laps and soon the rest of my teammates showed up. They said practice didn't really start until 3 p.m. Most of them had 2 p.m. classes, so they usually didn't get there until around 3:15. So maybe I wouldn't miss many English classes after all.

The pile in that dorm corner grew
with paper, scraps, pizza boxes,
hamburger wrappers, popcorn bags,
and soda cans. The mess only multiplied.

We took infield and outfield practice. Everybody got five swings against real pitching and practiced two bunts, running out the last one as fast as possible. After practice, we counted all the balls, making sure that if we started with 27, we ended with 27. That was one of my jobs, making sure whatever equipment we started with at the beginning of the practice, we had at the end.

Then Coach called us all together. "Now boys, our first game is this Friday. We've just come back from the spring trip. We were 9 and 2. Let's keep it going. And boys, I think this team is going to be a winner."

"That's all," he said, and we ran back towards the gym. I stopped for a few minutes and sat down on the side of the fountain, and as I was taking off my spikes, I started talking to my friends under the umbrella.

"Hey guys! I'm the starting shortstop. I'm hitting good and am excited about our first conference game Friday. I'm ready." The girl and the boy under the umbrella just looked at me.

59

I had made the pitcher throw two strikes.
Now I had to come through
and get on base.

I headed over to the training room to see Doc about a little stone bruise I had on my glove hand. As he looked it over, I noticed the gymnasts were climbing over the homemade climbing board; basketball players were doing pull-ups on the bars; guys were being treated with hot and cold packs and being massaged on the three training tables. Two fellows had their elbows in a little whirlpool, and one of our pitchers, who had been hit by a ball that knocked his glove off, was holding a bag of ice.

Spring football practice was under way, and Doc started telling the big, big guy I met the first day, "All right Antoine, you're the winner of our Johnson and Johnson Award today." I hoped that I would never get that award, but before the baseball season was over, I won the Johnson and Johnson Award twice.

Homework? First, Order a Pizza

That night, after the dorm meeting, I gathered all my books on my desk and started reading. Jerry came in late from work. He was pooped and had to go to bed.

"Aren't you going to study?" I asked.

"Nah man, I don't have to study; I get good grades."

"Man, I wish I was like that."

"Wanna order a pizza?" he asked.

I said, "Yeah, that sounds good."

So he went down to the end of the hall, made a call, and within

15 minutes we had a pizza from the Purple Mousetrap restaurant. It was great! When we were through I asked him, "What do we do with the box?"

"Throw it out the window or throw it in the corner."

I threw it in the corner. For the rest of the quarter, the pile grew and grew with paper, scraps, pizza boxes, hamburger wrappers, popcorn bags, and soda cans. We would pitch some of it from time to time, but the mess only seemed to multiply. Eventually, we got company. One night towards the end of the term, we were studying and heard scratching. We slowly turned around, and back in the corner were two mice chewing on some old pieces of pizza and hamburger. We watched for a minute, shrugged, and went back to the books.

CHAPTER NINE

Playing in Real Time: First Conference Game

OUR FIRST CONFERENCE game was against Illinois State. I was the lead-off man and shortstop. We had a great infield. We had a senior, Dick, playing first base. Itch was the second baseman – he and I had become good friends. His real name was Rich, but nobody ever called him that. Ken played third base.

We were in the IIAC, the Illinois Inter-Collegiate Athletic Conference, and most of the schools were from Illinois, Michigan, and Indiana. We would play a game every Friday and a double-header on Saturday against the same team. Occasionally we would play a non-conference game on Tuesday. So, we had practice on Monday, Wednesday, and Thursday, a regular game on Tuesday, a game Friday, and two games on Saturday.

Curveball, Fastball and 'Strike Two!'

I loved leading off. I almost always took the first two pitches as I felt confident no one could throw the ball by me. The first pitch was a curve ball. The umpire called a strike. The second pitch was a fastball. I didn't swing and the umpire called, "Strike two!" Suddenly, I was in the hole – two strikes, no balls, the first man at bat in our first Conference Game. I felt comfortable though. I felt confident. It was where I wanted to be. I had made the pitcher throw two strikes. Now I had to come through and get on base. I pulled the third pitch down the third baseline for a foul ball. Still, no balls and two strikes. The next pitch came high and inside and knocked me down,

and the following pitch was a curve that slid outside for ball two.

Though I was confident, I was also a very restless batter. I constantly moved the bat forward and back, forward and back. For this reason, one of my baseball nicknames was "Tiger Man," along with many other names I won't mention.

Anxious to hit one, I fouled the next pitch straight back to the screen. The following pitch was in the dirt. Now the count was 3 and 2. The next pitch was low. I let it go by. The umpire called it a ball. I was on first base!

Itch batted next and bunted down the third baseline. It was a perfect bunt, and the third baseman came in to field it. I went to second base, but on the third baseman's throw to first base, I noticed the third baseman wasn't going back to third base, so I headed for it. The third baseman forgot about me, so I rounded second base and kept going. By the time the third baseman realized I was going to third base, it was too late – I was safe without a play. Itch made a perfect sacrifice.

Freddie was the next batter. He was a big left-handed center fielder. He hit the first pitch about 400 feet, straight to center. The field wasn't fenced, so in most ballparks that would have been a big, big home run, but the center fielder drifted back and back and back and caught it. I only needed to tag third base and walk home for the first run of the game. We won that game and the next two. We took three games out of three, and as far as Coach was concerned, we were on our way to winning the Conference.

Back in St. Louis

The next game was on Tuesday, a non-conference game against St. Louis University. We were playing in my hometown. My dad and mom both worked, so they couldn't come to the game. My brother Tom was in school, so he couldn't come either. I was disappointed, but my mind was on the game. We went down 1-2-3 the first inning. In fact, I struck out my first time up. In the first inning, SLU loaded the bases with no-body out. The fourth batter hit a bullet between first and second. Itch dove for the ball, caught it on the first bounce, rolled over and threw to me at shortstop. I tagged second base, with my right foot pivoting and threw to first for a double play. The man on third base scored. They were winning 1-0.

I could feel my thigh burn with pain as I slid.
The important thing was that I was safe
and two runners scored.
The bad news was that I could
hardly lift myself off the ground.

It stayed that way until the top of the seventh inning. Our eighth batter walked. Our ninth batter, the pitcher, sacrificed him to second base. I was up next. The first pitch was the slowest ball I had ever seen. Sometimes, when you're batting, the ball seems small and fast; some-times, it's big and slow. This ball was like a grapefruit. It came in on a platter and said, "Hit me!" So I did. I hit it between the right fielder and center fielder for a triple, scoring our man on second base. It was a tied ballgame.

Itch came up to bat. Batting left-handed, he pulled one fair, over the first baseman's head, down the right-field line. I scored; he reached second base. Then we went crazy. We scored another seven runs any way we could. We ended up winning 8-1, maintaining the perfect record we'd held since we came back from our southern trip.

A 'Strawberry' Even Miss Ashley Couldn't Offer

Whenever I got suited up to play, I always – well, almost always – wore my sliding pads. Whenever I had to slide in a game, I could count on them to keep me from getting bruised, or worse, getting a bloody scratch or tear on my thigh, called a "strawberry." It's an ugly, swollen, red sore that can be very painful.

'Doc, why don't you just cut his leg off?'
a football player in the room hollered.

One day, I forgot to wear my sliding pants, and in the third inning of another conference game, I slid hopelessly into third base after hitting a straight shot between the right fielder and center fielder. I realized, as I was sliding, that the surface was rocky. I could feel my thigh burn with pain as I slid. The important thing was that I was safe and two runners scored. The bad news was that I could hardly lift myself off the ground.

Coach came right over to make sure I was okay.

"Do you still want to play?" he asked.

"Of course. I'm fine."

66

I wasn't, but no baseball player wants to be a quitter. So I played the entire game. We won 7-2. I went three for four. But I was in pain from the time I slid into third base until the time I limped into the training room.

"Hardy, what are you doing in here?"

I said, "Doc, I did something stupid."

"Well, what did you do?" Doc asked.

I turned sideways so he could see the side of my left leg. The strawberry was cut open a little bit and was oozing.

"Wow! What an A+ strawberry! I'll tell you what. Let me make sure it's clean and rub it down a little with alcohol. . ." Doc said.

"Are you crazy? I'll go through the roof." When he touched me with the light towel that he had put alcohol on, I thought I was going to take off.

"YIKES!" I yelled.

Doc had me lie there for about an hour with an ice bag on my thigh. After that, he said,

"Okay Hardy, here's what we're gonna do. Tomorrow, before practice, I want you to come in here. I want to take a look at your strawberry to see if it's healing and if the wound is closed."

"Doc, why don't you just cut his leg off?" a football player in the room hollered.

I winced. But I laughed anyway, and everybody in the room cracked up. Doc treated my wound with salve and gauze, and taped it up.

"Okay, I think you've had it today. Go home. Don't do any sliding on it tonight."

"Thanks, Doc!"

"Oh, Hardy," Doc called out. "Congratulations – you have just won the Johnson and Johnson Award," he said.

"But Doc, I was hoping to get through the whole season without winning it."

"Well, too bad," he said. "That was the dumbest move any of the athletes pulled today."

Ouch!

Visualization — and Learning to Love Numo

One thing I was always up for was to hit and bunt, so I began a visualization ritual once the season started. Every day after practice or after a game, I would go up to the second floor across the hall from the gymnasium. A little room up there had a large mirror on the wall. Every day I would take my bat up to that room, stretch a little, touch my toes, and do 20 push-ups. I would face the mirror like it was the pitcher. Then I would take 100 swings, making sure my hands stayed back and my weight didn't move forward, all the time making up possible pitches:

Here's a high pitch at the letters, a low pitch at the knees, inside and high, outside and low, right down the middle.

Adjusting my hands for each imaginary pitch, I made sure that wherever I thought the ball was going to go, the fat part of the bat would go over the plate. I'd tell myself that the other pitcher was good, but he was not going to throw anything by me – a curve ball, a drop, or a sinker. He had a pitch he would throw that looked like it was going to hit me, but then it would move over the inside corner of the plate, or he'd send a pitch to the outside of the plate to be a ball. I worked on every possible kind of pitch I could.

Each time, I'd try to take the same type of swing, directing my hands so the bat would hit the ball at an angle towards the right field side, center field, or the left side of the ball field, depending on where I imagined the ball was headed.

By the time I finished the ritual, I was pooped. But the 100 swings every day helped me learn and get stronger.

For some reason, my back bothered me as the season progressed. Before practice, Doc or one of the assistant trainers would rub some pink goo on my back that tingled. Numotizine, an ointment also used on horses to help them get over their ailments, worked great on me, relieving swelling and pain. After applying the Numotizine, they'd add gauze and tape up my back. Then, after practice, off with the tape and gauze, on to the shower and then into the whirlpool.

The monstrous, seven-foot whirlpool, oddly shaped like a body with outstretched arms and legs, was all silver metal and could hold a 300-pound football player or a 150-pound baseball player like me.

Each person who used the whirlpool had to fill it, empty and clean it when they finished. I'd fill it up so when I got in and laid down and put my head on the headrest, I was completely submerged in warm, rotating water. My back would tingle and burn while in the whirlpool, but it felt really good. Within two weeks my back was better. Even after I stopped using the Numo, I still kept filling, soaking, emptying, and cleaning the whirlpool at least three times every week, rain-out or ballgame.

CHAPTER TEN

School Daze

ALONG WITH ALL the practices, games, lining the field, watering the infield, and making sure the bases, bats and balls were accounted for, I also had to keep going to classes.

After the first couple of weeks, I really started enjoying college. Going to classes with 10-minute breaks in between was cool. I'd walk around campus with my briefcase filled with weights to strengthen my wrists, going from one class to another, saying hello to everybody, and looking at all the pretty girls. Then, every day at 2 p.m., I was ready for baseball.

But Did You Read The Book?

I was really enjoying college until the academic tests started. I never tested well. My first few tests weren't bad, but then there were midterms. I can't believe some of the questions that were asked on the exams. In my English class, one question had several parts:

- **Name the title of the book we were reading**
- **Name the author**

- **Name all the parts of the Index**
- **How many pages were in the book**

I had no idea why anyone would ask those kinds of questions, and I didn't know the answers. It turned out nobody else did, either. No one passed.

The English instructor spent the entire hour discussing how important details were. He said if we really didn't know all the details on the book's subject, then reading the book didn't mean anything. We needed to know who wrote it and when, what the title was, everything in the index, and whether it was a short or long book. I guess it made sense. On the second test the following week, he didn't ask any questions like that. All the questions were right out of the book. If you read the book, you scored well. Well, I didn't read the whole book. I got a C- on that test.

One question on my English mid-term test was obscure. We were studying Chaucer. The question was: "What was the name of Chaucer's horse?" Only one person got the name of the horse correct – Zephyr. Who knew? In those days we didn't have Google.

I was really worried about that class. It was hard, and I had missed one Tuesday class when we went to St. Louis to play St. Louis University. I also missed a Friday class when we were out of town playing Indiana State. When I got my grade back from the mid-term, I got a C- with a note that read, "See me!"

When I approached the dour instructor – whose name, unbelievably, was Dr. Rainbow –

I asked why he wanted to see me.

"Well, it's about your missing class," he said. "I told you I won't tolerate anyone missing class, and you've missed two of my classes already. Why?" I told him I was on the baseball team, and we had ball games.

"That's no excuse. I told you, if you were a jock, you should find another English class."

I just looked at him.

"Well, don't you have anything to say?" he asked.

"Yes, sir! I'll do everything I can to get a good grade."

"Well you're not starting off very well. If I were you, I'd get out of my class."

'Hardy, remember if you tell Coach
you are going to do something, you do it,
because it works both ways.
He expects us to give 110 percent,
and he'll do the same,' Itch said.

That day at practice, I told Coach that everything was going great except for my English class with Dr. Rainbow. He asked me what was wrong. I told him, and he said to keep him informed.

I found out later that Coach had a little talk with Dr. Rainbow. They were good friends, but Dr. Rainbow told Coach he didn't appreciate people missing his class. Coach must have said something back to him because from then on, my English grades got better, and Dr. Rainbow seemed to be somewhat happier with me. I also thought I did really well on the final, but in the end, I only got a C in the class.

CHAPTER ELEVEN

A 'Real Straight Shooter'

AFTER PRACTICE ONE day, Itch and I decided to walk, instead of jog, back to the locker room. As we were walking and taking in the SIU campus, Itch asked, "How are you getting along with Coach?"

"Great! He is really a straight-shooter, isn't he?"

"I don't think you'll find anybody who is more of a straight-shooter," Itch said. "His handshake is gold. Whatever he tells you he is going to do, he does."

"I know. Last summer, when he scouted me up in St. Louis, we were both sitting on the backdrop of his station wagon when he asked me to come to Carbondale on a scholarship to get educated and play baseball.

"I had gotten some scholarship offers in music, but I really wanted to play ball. So I told him yes. The paperwork showed up in November, and that was it. Everything was taken care of, and it was all done on a handshake."

"That's exactly right," Itch said. "You don't need to sign a whole lot of paperwork. If he tells you something, that's it. Hardy, remember, if you tell him you are going to do something, you do it, because Coach works both ways. He expects us to give 110 percent, and he'll do the same."

I said, "Do you remember when we were down in New Orleans on the spring trip, and we started following him through a real rich part of town? He turned down one street, and he pointed to some pretty flowers and clapped. We were all making fun of Coach when we got out and clapped, as he always wanted us to see the pretty houses, great decorations, and the beautiful flowers and plants . . ."

Itch interrupted.

"But you know Hardy, that's a part of education, and Coach wants to make sure, above all, we know that even though we are on a baseball/working scholarship, the education we get is more important than playing and winning games, winning the conference, batting .300, or winning a championship."

"That's what it seems like," I said. "He wants us to play the best we can and win, but if we don't win, and we played our best, he's not going to come down on us. But if we didn't play our best, I'll bet he could come down on us pretty hard whether we won or lost."

"And, you know," Itch said, "he would rather play by the rules and lose than do something stupid and win."

"I don't understand what you mean."

"Well, for example, let's say we're batting, and a man is on first base, with no outs. He's going to try to bunt that man to second base or, if we're winning, he might do a hit-and- run. But he's not going to have that teammate of ours on first base steal second unless he feels confident that he's going to get down there safe.

"When he's coaching third base, if he thinks the play is going to be close he's going to have our man slide in," Itch continued. "If he thinks there's going to be a close play at home plate, chances are he's going to stop the man at third. Better to be safe and still in the game than risk the possibility of getting an out and ending the game.

"Coach plays his odds and he expects us to do the same. At the same time, he expects us to get good grades."

"Well," I said, "I've been having some problems with my English instructor, but other than that, I think I'm maybe not going to get great grades, but good grades. If I can get a couple of As, a couple Bs and maybe a couple Cs, I'll be satisfied."

"All of us can't be geniuses," Itch said. "Just pass. Coach will not keep you on the team if you don't pass your classes."

You never knew when a shoe, towel,
bat, baseball, football, or tennis ball
might come flying past you, or worse, hit you in the head.
It was crazy fun.

"Coach has helped a lot of people," Itch added. "If he finds out that students can't make it through school financially, he has gotten them jobs working at the university, whether it's umpiring, cleaning floors or locker rooms or working around the Intramural Office or some other office on campus. They were then able to earn enough money to stay at Carbondale. Many times, the students don't even know he got the jobs for them. He's not someone who needs to be told "thanks." He'd rather you thank him by giving 110 percent."

CHAPTER TWELVE

Dave and the 'Animals'

WHENEVER I GOT ready in the gym for baseball, the jocks were always in the locker room – track guys, wrestlers, tennis, spring football players, and others. The locker room was noisy and dangerous. You never knew when a shoe, towel, bat, baseball, football, or tennis ball might come flying past you, or worse, hit you in the head. It was crazy fun.

One day in the gym, I heard somebody yell, "Hardy!" I looked up. It was Dave Mullane, from Central High School in St. Louis, a rival high school of Beaumont, my high school. He weighed in at 320 pounds. Standing next to him was Gene, 325 pounds, and next to him was Jerry, 365 pounds. They all played football at Central where their title was "The One-Thousand-Pound Line."

"Hey Dave, Gene, Jerry! How you doin'?

"We're doing great. "We'll come over and see you sometime."

Oh brother, I hope not, I thought. They were wild. They could sit on me and kill me, or break my door down and cause a lot of trouble. We could also have a lot of fun, but the trouble would be worse. I could lose my scholarship hanging around with those guys. I wanted to see them, but...

Dave Remembers

"They called me 'The Animal' because I was big and strong and loved to play football and tackle people," Dave reminded me last year. "We were a bunch of crazy guys. We were rowdy and wild, partied, and tended bar after football season. You were a good baseball player and were always joking around with us, but you were a smart guy who didn't drink. So you weren't as wild as we were. But those were good times."

I told Dave that as much as they tortured me with their brutish ways, I had to admit we had fun.

Ladies who lunch

Every day, we would join the women and have lunch at Woody Hall. Eating at Woody Hall was special. Woody Hall was an on-campus, three-story high, all-girl dormitory, about a five-minute walk from Dowdell Halls. The only fellows who got to eat there were the jocks from Dowdell Halls. So we pretty much got anything we wanted to drink and eat, especially extra desserts from the girls who were always dieting. Dave, Gene, and Jerry would sit at a table by themselves, chowing down everything they could get their hands on. The girls would come by and slowly and carefully leave their desserts on the Thousand-Pound-Line's table and then move away quickly. They never knew if The Animals were going to thank them or bite their heads off. That was fine with me – that meant the girls spent more time talking and flirting with me. I knew one thing – The Animals weren't sexy.

*I slowly opened the door and looked in.
The floor was filled with shattered bottles
and busted cans of beer.*

Hardy to the Rescue

One day, Dave and Gene got into a tussle and started wrestling in the lunchroom. They knocked over a bunch of tables and then fell on one and broke it. The rest of the guys told them to get out of there before they got into trouble.

Later that night, I had a knock on my door. I opened the door and there stood the football coach.

"Are you Hardy?"

"Yes, sir!"

"I'm Coach Franzel, the football coach. We've got a problem. We can't get Dave and Gene out of their room. We know they're drinking beer. It's against policy to drink beer on campus. Every time we try to go in, they throw a beer bottle at the door."

"Well, how can I help?"

"Dave's been yelling that he wants to talk to Hardy. Will you go talk to him?"

"Sure, Coach. Let's see what I can do."

So we walked over to Dowdell Halls 5. The coach motioned to Dave and Gene's room, the first door on the right. I knocked on the door and – CRASH! – a couple of bottles broke on the other side of the door.

"Hey Dave, it's Hardy," I said through the door.

"I'm going to eat you! I'm going to kill you! I'm going to mangle you!" Dave yelled out.

"Dave, your coach is out here, and he said you were asking for me. Now remember, YOU were asking for ME. I'm a baseball player, and you know I'm a little guy. If you end up hurting me, you're going to get in big trouble, lose your scholarship, and go back to St. Louis. Do you want that?"

Another crash, and two more bottles hit the inside of the door.

"Okay," I said. "Here's the deal. I know how drunk you are, but I'm gonna come in there, and if you guys throw bottles at me or hurt me, your coach and mine are going to be steamed. And you are going to lose your scholarship. No more SIU football."

"When you come in here, Hardy, I'm going to eat you! I'm going to break you into pieces!" Dave said, growling.

"One. . ." I began. Several bottles busted up against the door.

"Two. . ." More bottles smashed.

"Three. . ." It was quiet.

I slowly opened the door and looked in. The floor was filled with shattered bottles and busted cans of beer. Dave was lying in shorts in one bunk, and Gene was on the other bunk. Each had a large quart of beer. They had unscrewed the legs off the top bunk and broken the beds apart so both beds were down on the floor. Dave was still growling.

"I'm going to kill you and everybody out in the hall."

I ignored his drunken blather.

"Now, we'll get the rest of the fellows in the dorm to clean your room so everything is back to where it was, but you've got to get out of here, and you've got to do it now. You've got to go with the coach," I said.

"Screw you, Hardy! We're throwing you out the window."

"Dave, you can't do that; you'll lose your scholarship. Now, let's go!"

"Screw you!"

"Dave, Gene, do you want to go back to St. Louis?"

"Yeah. I wanna go back and get drunk in St. Louis," Dave shouted.

"No, you don't. Don't both of you want to play football?"

"No! I want to drink," Dave whined.

"Yeah, I want to play football, but I want to drink too," Gene said.

"You can't do both. You either play football or you drink; but, if you drink, you go back to St. Louis. Now get out of here. Stand up! Put your pants on! Put a shirt on and let's go!"

I opened the door. A bunch of guys were out in the hall, waiting to see what was going on. Slowly, Dave and Gene dressed and came out, looking at everybody.

"Get out of my way! I'll kill you! I'll eat you! I'll break you apart!" Dave snarled at them.

Everybody, including the football players, backed up.

They walked outside. The coach was there with his assistant coach; both were big and mean. The coach spoke up.

"Okay, let's go. We're going to the President's office."

Dave and Gene said nothing.

In the end, they were expelled, but only for three days. Everyone, it seemed, was afraid of them but me. I'd have tossed them out for three months – or longer.

Hangin' at Carrie's

During the spring quarter, most of the athletes went out on Friday and Saturday nights, except the track, tennis, cross-country and baseball guys, who were playing their seasonal games. None of the baseball players went out past curfew on Friday nights because we always had a double-header on Saturday. If we went out, we'd go on Saturday night.

The football players all had curfews during spring football training, but that never fazed Dave, Gene, and Jerry. They were always out – out cold, actually – most of the time waking up outside a bar on a Saturday morning. There were a couple of bars outside of town where the students went to dance, drink and socialize. Carrie's, a bar about five miles outside of Carbondale, was the most popular. One night, Dave was outside after leaving the bar when a dog came out of nowhere, bit Dave in the leg, and held on. That was a big mistake for the dog. Dave picked up the dog and bit it back, in the neck. The dog howled and took off, never to be seen again.

As crazy as he acted with that dog, Dave was just as brutish with the ladies. He was in the bar one night, and when he went to sit on a stool, a girl said, "Hey, that's my stool."

"Hey broad, it's mine. Now leave me alone or I'll punch your lights out!" he said.

She went to smack him, but he grabbed her hand. He then took his beer bottle and busted it over his own head and growled at her. "Whose stool is it, broad?"

She caved. "Yours," she said, and quickly walked away. After witnessing Dave's outrageous behavior, she must have felt very lucky he didn't bust the beer bottle over *her* head. Yes, he was a real ladies' man.

In All Her Glory: Big Mary

Dave's idea of a fine woman was Big Mary – the coarse, heavyset, big-breasted bartender at the Rat Hole Bar.

One day, I bumped into him, and he insisted I meet her.

"Mary!" he shouted as we walked into the bar. "I want you to meet a buddy of mine from St. Louis – Hardy!"

"Hey, Hardy! How you doin'?"

I stared. She was the accident you couldn't look away from.

"I'm good," I said.

"You know what, Big Mary? Hardy's a virgin!"

"Are you a virgin?" she asked me.

"Well... I guess so."

"Let me show you something," she said and flipped out her left boob and laid it on the bar. I backed up and almost fell over.

"Well, if that's what happens to you when you just see one of them, do you think I should take 'em both out?" she asked.

I couldn't have stomached it. "No, one is enough for right now."

From then on, Big Mary called me "Virgin Hardy."

I saw her again one night in Dave and Gene's dorm room. I had walked over to see what they were up to. I banged on the door.

"Who's there? Leave me alone. We're busy," Dave said.

"It's me, Dave. It's Hardy."

The door opened. He pulled me inside and closed the door.

"Dave, what's wrong?" And as I said that, I looked around and saw Big Mary, her large hips stuck in the window.

"Is she coming or going?" I asked. The windows were so low that normally you could get in or out of the windows with a little pull or push from someone helping you. Mary, with all her endowments, was the exception.

"I'm trying to go now," she said. "Virgin Hardy, can you help me? I don't want them pushing or pulling on me."

"Why don't you try to turn sideways? Lift your right hip up so you are angled."

As she did that, she started slowly sliding out the window. Then,

Dave and Gene pushed her out the rest of the way. She flopped down on the ground.

"What do I do now?" she asked.

"We don't care. Just get out of here," Dave said and slammed the window shut, leaving poor Mary on the ground.

Dave and Gene turned to me, and Gene asked, "So what did you want anyway? Why did you come over here bothering us?"

"You know, right now I really can't remember, but it was sure worth the trip," I said.

Knocked it off its hinges,

the door went flying forward,

hitting the floor. Dave was flying through the air.

Some time later, in the middle of the night, I was awakened by a banging on my door.

"It's me! I'm gonna kill you!"

Dave! You're drunk! Go back to your dorm," I yelled.

"If you don't let me in, I'm gonna knock this door down!"

"Dave, go back to your room or I'll call the coach! You don't want to lose your scholarship, do ya?"

That made him really mad, and he shoved the door, which exploded open.

Knocked it off its hinges, the door went flying forward, hitting the floor. Dave was sailing through the air. He landed on the door and banged his head. He was out cold and didn't move for the rest of the night. When my roommate and I got up the next morning, we just tip-toed around him, got dressed, and went to class. He came to at some point and left the room, leaving broken debris everywhere. At least he never knocked the door in again.

The Animals Go to School

The Animals didn't just act up in the dorms and in the bars, their antics showed up in the classroom, too. Dave was in my history class, and one day we were taking the mid-term exam. Dave was sitting in the very last row, next to the window. No one knew it, but he had dropped the test questions out the window so Fran, one of the women who worked in the Athletics Department, could write the answers for him. After a half-hour, she came back and spent ten minutes trying to get the paper back up to Dave, who was trying to reach out the back window without being seen by our instructor. Finally, she folded the paper into an airplane and flew it up to Dave. He grabbed it and turned in his answers with the rest of us.

The following week, our instructor said, "I would like to announce the person who had the highest score on the test. Would Dave Mullane please stand up?"

"I want to read all the questions and have you give the answers," Mr. Scott, the instructor, said. One by one, Mr. Scott read the questions, and Dave read the correct answers off his test paper.

Mr. Scott moved in for the kill.

"Dave, those are exactly the right answers, but could you please show your answer sheet to the class?"

Dave paled.

He turned the paper around so we could see his answers. They were typed! The rest of the class hand-wrote their answers. We all started laughing. Dave was a cheat and a dumb one at that!

"Would you please tell the class how you were able to type the answers when there are no typewriters in this room?" Mr. Scott asked.

Dave looked at Mr. Scott, then the class. "Well, last week there was a typewriter, and it was right on top of my desk."

"Dave, is that the truth?"

Dave said, "Yes sir!"

Mr. Scott just shook his head. And for some reason I could never figure out, Dave passed the class.

And So It Was...

For the next several years, Dave, Gene, and Jerry goofed off in school, drank, chased horrified girls, and clobbered people who got in their way.

They did this for maybe six years, but it seemed like ten years. They'd play one season, sit out two quarters, and return for summer school where they took basket-weaving, recreation, P.E., and safety. They would pass the classes, and then be eligible to play the next year. Even during the fall season, they remained incorrigible, drinking hard and playing football. And they'd flunk out again. I lost count of how many years it took them to graduate.

"Dave definitely liked his beer and did a lot of head-butting. It was his way of saying hello," Mike Pratt told me many years later. "But, you know, he was a great guy and would do anything for you. And he wasn't the only one who got into trouble. We all did things we probably shouldn't have done, mischievous things. It was just college fun." Mike, a lifelong star athlete who played college baseball with me, went on to become a great high school basketball and baseball coach before he retired in 2001.

CHAPTER THIRTEEN

Odd But True:
'The Little People'

.

THE THREE NON-JOCKS in Dowdell Halls 6 were short, wore big glasses, were blessed with brilliance, and they also got the only large room in the dorm to share. We called them "The Little People." They understood math, knew all the equations, and were powerhouses of knowledge in literature and history. They came in handy because they helped us all with our homework. And they seemed to like doing it. Even so, they were easy targets for ridicule, and some of the football players knew it. They'd punch a hole in the wall of The Little People's dorm room and send somebody's fist flying through it. The fist became a hand that would wave and disappear. Who knows what the three-some thought?

For the wrestlers, punching holes in walls was only mild torture. One day, while everyone was showering, several wrestlers grabbed The Little People, carried them naked out the back door of the dorm and dropped them down the stairs right in front of a group of married women. As soon as all three of The Little People were thrown down the steps, one of the football players locked the back door. The Little People scrambled around to get back in the door while the ladies were gasping, laughing, and applauding. Later, eight of the women's husbands came over demanding an apology from the wrestlers, but the wrestlers ran them off the grounds shouting obscenities and threats of bodily harm.

I, Pod.

One of the most fun people in the dorm was "Pod," who lived right across the hall from me. Pod thought of himself as good-looking, and he literally charmed the pants off the ladies. He would sneak girls in through the back door and right into his room.

They talked a bit and then were quiet.
At last we could hear them both moving
on the bed, and the bed springs
squeaking slowly and rhythmically.

One night at dinner, Pod bragged about expecting a girl over, and five of us decided to catch him in the act.

We got into the room right next to his. His bunk bed was right on the other side of the wall. We waited. Sure enough, we heard her voice, and then the door closed. They talked a bit and then were quiet. At last we could hear them both moving on the bed, the bed springs squeaking slowly and rhythmically, then faster and faster. Sue and Pod were moaning and groaning. He said, "Okay. Now!" and Sue cried out "Now! Now! Don't Stop!" He said, "Now!" She said, "Now!" And when he said, "It's happening!" the five of us yelled "Oooh Pod, we love you! We love you. Oooh Pod, we love you!"

Sue started screaming and ran out of the dorm. Pod banged on our door, yelling all kinds of obscenities. He finally left but never mentioned having any visitors again. We didn't care; we had gotten him good.

Duck, Duck, Goose, Goose...

Pod was always telling us about his hunting experiences. He would go into a game reserve close to campus, where you weren't allowed to hunt, and shoot ducks, geese, and anything else that moved. He would bring them back and sometimes hang the goose necks and heads on my door knob. I decided to get even. One day he came back with his ducks. He cut the heads off and left them on the steps outside the back door and walked away, saying he was going to have a duck dinner with friends.

After he was gone, I went outside, grabbed several of the duck heads, and picked the bloodiest one. I went to his room and tied the duck's bloody head upside down around the lightbulb string. Then, I closed all of Pod's curtains, taping everything closed so no light would come through. I went back across the hall to my room.

A couple of hours later, Pod came back and opened his door.

"What the...? You S.O.B.s! I'll kill you! Oh my God! I got blood all over me! Who did this?" Then I heard him stumble around in the dark and fall over a chair I left in the middle of the room.

He came banging on my door.

"Hardy! I know you're in there! I'm going to kill you!"

I smiled, stifled a laugh, and waited for him to move on.

He went raging up and down the halls. Nobody knew what he was talking about. I had acted alone. And what a triumph! I thought about how he must have jumped in the air when he grabbed that duck's head, and I laughed again. I nailed him good. I slept like a baby that night. And he never came around with his bloody ducks again.

CHAPTER FOURTEEN

W-O-M-B Radio

ONE NIGHT, AS I entered Dowdell Halls 6, I saw a crowd standing in the hall in front of my buddy Vic's room, 613. I could hear Vic using his best broadcasting voice. Somehow he had hooked up a radio-type short wave unit that broadcasted about two miles in circumference. Once in awhile, he'd turn on the radio station he called WOMB and start talking to the women at Woody Hall. As I neared the crowd of laughing jocks and even the Three Little People, I could see Vic talking with a guy named Jim Minton who was sitting next to Vic and the equipment.

"What kind of information should we be sharing with those good-looking babes at Woody Hall tonight?" Vic asked Jim.

The Saluki cop said it was time for us to go,
but just then, one bra came sailing
out a window, and then another, and
another, and another...

"The dorms we live in are great, and we'd like to have the girls come in to Dowdell Halls," Jim said.

"But," Vic said, "girls can't come into Dowdell Halls, and we can't go into Woody Hall. They are off limits."

"Well, maybe we can kind of sneak 'em in one evening and sneak 'em out a few hours later. Our rooms are a mess, beds need to be made, floors can be cleaned, and we need some real nice pictures on the wall. The gals in Woody Hall are the best – not only the best looking, but they'd do a great job shaping up each of our rooms."

"What would they get in return?" Vic asked.

'We will have something special for them," Jim said, and the guys in the background hooted.

Vic and Jim laughed, and Vic turned the siren on.

"Oops, the cops are coming," he said, "and we have to sign off. Coming up next week we're all coming over to serenade you at Woody Hall, and we want your bras in return. Take off your bras, come to the window, and throw them down to us. That will make a great evening. So this is your buddy Vic signing off. You're listening to WOMB. W-O-M-B. We're outta here. Adios!"

A Hundred Thousand Bras on the Wall...

The following Monday, Vic was on the air again.

"Hello girls, this is Vic. We're coming over tonight. We'll be there in 30 minutes, so be prepared – we want you to give us the best show you can, and we want to leave with as many bras as we can – one for each of us. We each want bras to take back and hang up on our walls."

He signed off, and we walked over to Woody Halls. We were going to have a good time. But just as we got to Woody Halls, about six Saluki cops showed up. One of the cops came up to Tony, a big football player. "We know what you're going to do, making these girls take their bras off, and it's illegal," the cop said.

"It's not illegal," Tony argued. "We're not going to bang on the doors, we're just going to serenade the girls. And if they throw their bras down to us, is that really illegal?"

The Saluki cop gave up. "I guess it's not illegal," he said.

Then, many of the windows at Woody Hall opened, and the girls were hanging out and yelling, "Where's that serenade?" We got excited and began chanting:

> *"We're the men of Dowdell Halls,*
> *we're jocks who catch, throw, and hit the balls.*
> *Now we're here for you to cheer, and*
> *in return we want your brassieres.*
> *"Throw them out! Throw them out! Throw them out!"*

The girls were waving and yelling, "Sing some more! Sing some more!" But we just kept clapping and looking up at them. The Saluki cop said it was time for us to go, but just then, one bra came sailing out a window, and then another, and then another, and another. One coed stood tall, took off her bra, and threw it out. More girls stood tall, took off their bras, and threw them out. Then the windows went down, and the shades were drawn. We all went back to Dowdell Halls with a lot of bras, and for the rest of the term, everybody had at least one bra hanging on their wall. What a night! We thought Vic was terrific for putting on the show. Nobody got in trouble for the evening, but the next day, city cops came in and confiscated Vic's radio paraphernalia. And that was it for WOMB.

But that wasn't it for Vic. One night I woke to the bang of a shotgun right outside my door. Because my room was at the very end of the hall, and right next to the outside door, the gunshot was louder in my room than the other rooms further down the hall. I opened the door only to see Vic standing naked in the open door with his shotgun. "Dammit, I missed!" he said. He had been shooting at ducks flying over. Well, that got him kicked out of school for a week. But he was right back on the football field after that.

A Hundred Bottles of Beer—*In* the Wall?

One night after the bra party, I came home, walked into our dorm, and it was very quiet. Spooky. Nobody was around. I walked down to the end of the hall and put my key in the door, turned it, grabbed the doorknob, and pushed in. The door wouldn't open. I pushed a little bit harder, then harder still. The door opened a crack, and I could see several guys bunched together on one side of the room.

"Hardy, don't make any noise. We're drinking in your room," somebody said.

"What do you mean you're drinking in my room? You can't drink in the dorm!" I shouted.

"Yeah, everybody knows you don't drink, so we came down to your room for our beer party. No one will find us here."

"You guys gotta get out!"

"Nope, we're not gonna get out until we're finished drinking."

I never came home again to find anybody
in my room drinking beer.

The door opened a little bit more and I could see 12 guys in my room – four on my bunk, four on Jerry's, one on top of each desk and one in each chair in front of the desk. They were all drinking Coors.

"Where did you guys get the beer?"

"Don't tell me you don't know about the hidden hole in your wall," one of them said.

"What?"

Tony, the football player, came over and kind of tapped on the inside wall on the far side of my door. An area about 18 inches wide and 12 inches deep just kind of dropped down and there was space between the wall facing me and the wall on the opposite side from the hallway. Inside were cans of Coors.

"We've been storing beer in here the whole year," Pete said. The resident counselor would never think about looking in your and Jerry's room because you guys don't drink or smoke."

Between a Rock and a Hard Place

"Well, you guys can't keep this up. You've got to get the beer out of here."

"Just cool it! Don't get excited. Nobody's gonna find out. We'll keep it a secret. And you Hardy, have to keep it a secret because if it doesn't stay a secret, you could get kicked out of school."

They were right. They had me.

"You have two minutes to get out of the room," I said.

They all walked out of the room very quietly, walked out the back door of Dowdell 6 and into the night. As they were leaving, Tony closed up the little shelf in the wall so all you saw was a flat wall.

I never came home again to find anybody in my room drinking beer. But I began to wonder what drinking was all about.

Straight, no chaser

> *'You're gonna get drunk tonight,*
> *and you're not going to be*
> *a virgin anymore,' Dave said.*

One Sunday night, I was in my room and had studied as much as I could. Just as I was thinking I needed a break, there was a loud pounding on my door. Naturally, it was Dave.

"Hardy! Where are ya? Open the door!"

I opened the door and looked at Dave. "What's up?"

"Hey! Why doncha take a walk with me? We're going over to Sin City." Sin City was a trailer court right off campus, pretty close to Dowdell Halls; they called it Sin City because there was always a lot of drinking and partying going on.

"You know I've never been drunk, and I don't want to get drunk," I told Dave.

"No, you're gonna get drunk tonight, and after tonight, you're not going to be a virgin anymore."

"Ah, forget it," I said, but I had to admit I was curious. So I changed my mind.

"Okay, I'll come with ya."

We walked through campus to the trailer courts and stopped in front of a trailer. We knocked on the bottom of the door because there were no steps up. Somebody must have stolen the steps. A good-looking co-ed answered the door and said,

"Dave! Come on in." We had to climb up and in the door. Dave introduced me to Sherry and Betty who were roommates.

We sat around and talked for a while. Then Dave said, "Okay ladies! Here's the deal, we're going to get Hardy drunk. He's never been drunk before, and he's a virgin. There was a large, half-gallon bottle of Roma wine sitting on a table next to the bed. "Okay now, if you're gonna drink, we're all gonna drink and we're all gonna get drunk," Dave said.

So, everybody took a glass of Roma wine, and we started drinking.

It tasted awful – very bitter, just terrible. I drank a glass and told them, "Nothing's going on. I don't feel a thing. Forget it! I'm getting out of here."

The girls said, "No, no, no! Keep drinking, keep drinking." So, I had another glass and another glass, just like it was water, each in one gulp, but still felt nothing. So I kept drinking, one glass after another.

I guess an hour went by, and I still felt sober.

"I think I'm going go back to the dorm," I said. I stood up, and WOW! Was I loaded! I couldn't feel my legs or my fingers. My chest was pounding, my head was spinning and I immediately fell back into my chair.

Everyone was laughing. "Come on over here and sit on the bed next to me," Sherry said.

"I don't think I can make it over there. I don't feel good. I think I'd better get out of here."

Flying High

I got up slowly. The two girls on the bed looked like they were flying in the air. I was flying too. Dave was laughing, but it was like an echo – I couldn't hear real well, and I couldn't see either. I fell back against the door, found the handle, opened the door and bolted, but I forgot the concrete steps weren't there, and fell straight into the mud. I noticed it was raining, but the fall didn't hurt. Nothing hurt.

I don't know how I got back to the dorm, but the next thing I knew, I was standing in the lobby with Dave holding me up.

"Lemme go!" I shouted.

He did, and I immediately fell on the floor. I was soaked – my shoes, my pants, my shirt, everything was filled with mud. My face was completely covered with mud. Dave pulled me back up and carried me down the hall to 624.

"What happened to Hardy?" a guy standing nearby asked.

"I got him real drunk," Dave said.

Shaken, Not Stirred

When we got down to my room, my roommate was there, along with The Little People, Pod, and Vic. They could tell I was gassed. I took my clothes off right there, eased into the shower, dried off, and threw on a pair of undershorts and a t-shirt. When I got back to my room, the guys hoisted me up to the top bunk. I lay there while everybody laughed. My head was spinning, and my stomach churned.

My roommate was sitting on the bottom bunk bed right underneath me, but I didn't know he was there. I leaned over and puked all over his head. I thought he was going to kill me, but he just ran down the hall and jumped in the shower, clothes and all. When he came back, he was soaked and everybody was laughing.

The last things I remembered that night were the room spinning, the guys laughing, the two girls floating in the air, and my roommate screaming at me over and over.

And then, nothing.

The next morning I had such a vicious headache, I didn't even want to open my eyes. I finally pulled myself out of bed and suddenly realized I had my last test before finals in ROTC that morning. With a nasty wave of nausea, I headed for the bathroom and puked all over the floor while I sat on the john. I showered, cleaned up the mess, and went to take my final. I have no idea what questions were on the test, but somehow I must have passed because I got a B. Anyway, I didn't get drunk again.

CHAPTER FIFTEEN

The Beautiful Jan

Jan and I would have breakfast at Woody Hall,
walk around campus to the train station,
kiss, and say our good-byes.

THE WEEKEND ACTION started Friday nights. Trains from Chicago and St. Louis arrived, filled with girlfriends, boyfriends, and other visitors who came into Carbondale after dinner. We would all party Friday night, Saturday, and until Sunday afternoon when the trains left to take everyone home.

My girlfriend, Jan, who was from St. Louis, would take the train about once a month and visit me. I'd meet her at the station with about another 200 SIU students all waiting for their friends to arrive. Carbondale in those days was only about eight blocks long from campus to the center of town. Freshmen weren't allowed to have cars, so we walked everywhere we went.

The first time Jan came to visit me on the train, I made arrangements

for a place for her to stay in Woody Hall. On Saturday nights we would go to the Varsity Theater, which was jam-packed with students. It was so noisy you could hardly hear the movie, but it was a lot of fun. One weekend, the movie, *The Graduate*, was showing. Mrs. Robinson and Dustin Hoffman were great, and we all really liked the movie. The audience was cheering and applauding during the movie, and we couldn't hear well, but we had a great time.

Sunday mornings, Jan and I would have breakfast at Woody Hall. Then we would walk around campus and on to the train station, kiss and hug and say our good-byes. It was about a two-and-a-half-hour train ride between St. Louis and Carbondale. While riding home, Jan would always write me a letter on blue stationary. Two days later, I would get the letter telling me how much fun she had that weekend. In fact, so far I had gotten a letter from her every day from the first week I stayed at Coach's house.

How I Met the Beautiful Jan

In 1953, when I was 13, my parents moved to the north side of St. Louis, on Mimika Avenue near Goodfellow and Florissant Avenues. It was our first house. My aunt and uncle, Harry and Virginia, lived a couple of blocks away. Every other month, my mom and dad played cards with my aunt and uncle, along with their friends, Eddie and Gladys Levinn, and Mr. and Mrs. Lepping.

The first month we moved into our new house, the Leppings were hosting the card party. Usually, Tom and I stayed home, but Mr. Lepping told mom their 13-year-old daughter Kathy was having a party and I should come.

"Well, I won't know anybody," I said to my mother, who responded with remarkable prescience: "That's okay; you'll meet somebody."

So I went.

I remembered coming down the basement steps to the party and looking through the opening. I saw the most beautiful girl I had ever seen in my life. She had long, golden brown hair, styled in a pageboy, and bright rosy cheeks. She was wearing an orange sweater – boy, did she fill it out – an orange skirt, white bobby socks, and black and white saddle shoes. I came all the way down the steps and around the corner. It seemed like nobody else was there, only this girl. She had the biggest green eyes I had ever seen.

I was the only one without a date. Everybody introduced themselves and the beautiful, green-eyed girl said her name was Jan.

"We're playing a game called Flashlight. Do you know how to play it?" asked Dave, her date.

"No."

"We turn the flashlight off, and everybody kisses their date. Then, when I turn the flashlight back on, if one of the couples is not kissing, one of them gets the flashlight and gets to pick a new partner.

"Great," I said, "but I'm not dated up."

"I'll tell you what, you start with my date, Jan."

I looked at Jan, and Jan looked at me, and all I can tell you is that for the rest of the night – and little did we know, for the rest of our lives – we were never separated. Every time that flashlight was on we were kissing. When the flashlight wasn't on we were kissing.

During the party we had a couple of breaks, where the boys went with the boys, and the girls went with the girls. I didn't realize that during one of those breaks Jan told the other girls, "You stay away from Hardy. He's all mine."

From then on, I was.

CHAPTER SIXTEEN

Mid-season madness

*It started burning slowly, but then quickly spread
all throughout the infield. First down the third baseline,
then the first baseline, then out to the pitcher's mound,
until the entire infield was ablaze.*

Fire and Rain

It was now the middle of the season, and we had only lost two Conference Games. We were out in first place by four games over Western Illinois University and had a big weekend series coming up against them. It didn't start to rain until Friday afternoon during the fourth inning, and it was really just drizzle – at first. We made it through the entire game, winning 6-1. It poured Friday night and Saturday morning. With an all-dirt infield, a double-header on Saturday looked impossible. We'd have to make the games up sometime later in the year (We couldn't play Sundays, because of league rules). We certainly wanted to play on our home field rather than play someplace else later, especially not at Western Illinois University, where it was really tough to win. They were as tough at home as we were. We didn't want to play there. We wanted to play today – at home. About one hour before game time, the umpires got together with both coaches and said they didn't see how we could play. It was still raining, and the infield was sitting in water. Both teams wanted to play, but it looked like the umpires were getting ready to call the game.

Coach motioned to me and I ran over.

"Hardy, I want you to take four of the guys and go to my car. I have four gas cans in the trunk. Go fill them up."

I had no idea what he was thinking. Why would I fill up four gas cans? But I did what he said. I grabbed Itch, Jerry, and Ken and took off for the filling station.

When we got back to the ball field, the rest of our teammates were spreading sand on the infield from bags they had gotten out of our baseball barn. In mud up to their ankles, they were spreading the sand all over the infield. It looked like we were going to use almost all 30 of the 25-pound sandbags at one time on the muddy infield. The rain was now only a light sprinkle.

Coach walked over, lit a match,
and threw it into the gasoline patch
around home plate.

"Hardy, get some guys and empty the gasoline all over the infield," Coach ordered.

We didn't ask any questions. We just started dumping the cans of gas but were only able to cover home plate and a little bit out in front. Coach told us to go back and get more gasoline. We did, and came back, emptied those, and went back for more. By the time we finished, we had 20 gallons of gasoline spread all over the field.

The umpires and coaches told all the players and the people in the stands to back away from the infield. Coach walked over, lit a match and threw it into the gasoline patch around home plate. It started burning slowly, but then quickly spread down the third baseline, the first baseline, out to the pitcher's mound until the entire infield was ablaze. Coach had set a spectacular fire. The flames were 15 feet high, and the smoke was so thick you couldn't see the infield.

It burned and burned for about 35 minutes. When the fire was out, the infield looked like a disaster, but the water was gone and all that was left was sand and mud. The rain had stopped. A few minutes later, the umpires yelled, "We play ball in 30 minutes."

Both teams' players started playing catch, warming up, and stretching. I couldn't line the field or the batters boxes because, if I did, the lines would have gone every which way but straight. The mud was thick. I didn't know how we could play. Then, all of a sudden, the Man in Blue behind home plate yelled, "PLAY BALL!"

And we did! It was a great game, especially for hitters. As long as you hit the ball on the ground and not in the air, chances were you would make it to first base. You might have lost your spikes in the mud, but if you could get to first base, you had a base hit because the infielders either couldn't get to the ball, or when they got to it, the ball was covered with mud, and they couldn't throw it. By the time they wiped everything off, the hitter, who was sloshing to first base, made it there before the infielder could throw the ball.

Coach was always the magician – pulling the right thing
out of his hat at the right time.

Jerry, who was playing left field, and I each had five hits. Jerry went 5 for 6. He also made the last out of the game. We won both games, ensuring us a strong first-place position, way ahead of Western Illinois and most of the rest of the pack.

Bussie at the Wheel

During the season we traveled on an SIU bus from our campus to wherever we were playing and back. On each trip, we had the same bus driver, Terry, whom we dubbed "Bussie." Our coach's job was to get us to win, make sure we grabbed something to eat (if we could do it in one minute or less!), then take off and let Bussie do the rest.

Bussie was always ready. Whatever Coach wanted him to do, he did. He didn't speed, or at least he didn't tell Coach he was speeding. One day, we were on the one-way side of a turnpike headed to Western Michigan when Bussie missed the turnoff. He broke the news to coach who was seated up front.

"Well, why don't we turn around and go back?" Coach asked.

"Well, we can't do that, Coach; we are on a turnpike, and it is all one way."

Whether it was on our trips or at home, Coach was always the magician – pulling the right thing out of his hat at the right time.

"Bussie, pull over on the inside of the highway," he said. Coach then turned around and gazed into the back of the bus. He saw me and said, "Hardy, why don't you go to the top of the hill back there, where we just came from, and see if anybody is coming. If nobody's coming, let us know, and we'll go on the grass median back up to the top of the hill, and then we'll get on the right turnoff. Just keep letting us know if anyone is coming."

I ran to the top of the hill. Nobody was coming, so I waved and gave Bussie the go-ahead sign. Bussie made a U-turn in the grass median, pointing in the direction of where traffic would be coming. I turned again to see if anybody was coming and — yikes! – a police car was like 30 yards from me, coming to the top of the hill. I didn't know how to get Bussie's attention because I was so far away, and he was turning. The police car went right past me, up and over the hill. The police car's brakes screeched as soon as the cop saw our bus pulled off the inside median and headed back up the wrong side of the road. I came running back just about the time the police officer got out of the car and walked up to the bus.

"Officer, I can explain," I said.

"Well, I hope you can. In fact, you better be able to explain a lot and start right now. I've never seen a bus going the wrong way on the median of a turnpike."

Coach got out of the bus.

"Officer, you are just the person I was looking for."

We didn't expect Coach to go on the offensive. The cop didn't either. He stood there with his hands on his hips, looking at the bus headed the wrong way, looking at Coach, looking at me, and at the side of the bus that said *Southern Illinois University*.

"Why is that?" the cop asked.

"Well," Coach said reasonably, "we are on our way up to Western Michigan University for a baseball game, and we just missed the turn-off. I'm wondering if you could hold up traffic so we can go back to the turnoff." It was quite a request, and we cringed waiting for the answer.

But the officer just looked at Coach and said, "You know what? I think that's probably the right thing to do." The police officer got in his car and went up to the top of the hill. I jumped in the bus. The police officer stopped his car, got out, and waved for us to come up. We got back on the turnpike road, going the wrong way, and made it to our missed turnoff. Not one car came by. Coach had pulled off another miracle, and more were to come.

Her restaurant was not easy to find,
and it was like going through
Florida swampland to get there.

Eats: Ma Hale's No-Name Restaurant

Our times on the road were always adventurous. Once in awhile, we'd stumble across unusual places – ghost towns, tiny towns with one stop sign, greasy spoons, run-down neighborhoods, or palatial ones. But the great thing about the tiny towns we passed through on the way to games was the home-cooked meals you could get at the local restaurants. And so it was that we came to the tiny town of Grand Tower, Illinois. Grand Tower sits along one of the Mississippi River's narrowest points, across from the Missouri side of the river near Cape Girardeau, in the southeast corner of the state. Population in 1959: 41.

Some of the more seasoned players had been there before and raved about Ma Hale's cooking. At 90 years old, she was crack-whip sharp and always had a speech for the players while they were eating. Her restaurant was not easy to find, and it was like going through Florida swampland to get there. We found it in a rickety building with no sign, no name, no nothing but the seasoned ballplayers who all knew that this was the place.

Lip-Smackin' Good

Ma's specialty was fried chicken, and she served it with mashed potatoes, green beans, spinach, corn, salad, biscuits, butter, honey, and hot gravy. Cherry pie, apple pie, peach pie, and carrot cake beckoned, but you had to be a tough guy to handle it after all that chicken.

Coach had promised that we could stop and eat at Ma's if we won a game against Southeast Missouri State (which we did), so we headed for Grand Tower. With the coaches, the sports writer, and the team, we had 20 people. We all sat down at one long table, and the food started coming. I couldn't believe it. There were seven platters of fried chicken – breasts, legs, thighs, gizzards, necks – every part of the chicken was on the platters. We dug in! I didn't notice it then, but the seniors took their time eating. That's not how they ate all during the baseball season. We were always in a massive hurry to beat Coach, but today, the seniors and upperclassmen just took their time. But I was chowing down fast – grabbing chicken legs, chicken thighs, chicken breasts – you name it, and I gorged myself. I ate everything, the fixings, a piece of every pie, and a good slice of the carrot cake. I was full after 15 minutes, but I ate more, and when we got back on the bus, I polished off some extra chicken that I had stuffed in my pocket.

I had been so looking forward to Ma Hale's that I had almost forgotten about the game we won. As we headed back to Carbondale, I closed my eyes and replayed the game in my head...

From Carbondale, it was only about an hour ride to Cape Girardeau. We arrived at Southeast Missouri State at noon. The ballgame was to start at 3:00 p.m. We went into the locker room, got dressed, and went out to the ball field for practice. I knew some of the players on Cape's team from St. Louis. I had played against them either in high school or summer ball games. They were a good team. They looked good that day. Their hitters were jacking the ball over the fence during batting practice. Our big hitters looked fine too during batting practice.

We took infield and got ready to play. It was almost like it was magic. Everything we did went right. I went four for five – one single, two doubles, and a triple. I thought my one double was going to be a home run, but the scoreboard sticking up in the playing field stopped my shot for a home run. I hit it too hard. It ended up hitting the scoreboard, and the ball bounced almost directly back to the center fielder. It was close, with me sliding into second base, but the umpire called me safe.

I opened my eyes again about 15 minutes before we got back to Carbondale when Itch asked me how I liked Ma Hale's. I said I thought it was great, but that I was stuffed. He laughed and said, "That's what always happens. That's why you saw the upperclassmen just taking their time. The rookies always eat fast and a lot, then, about the time we get back to Carbondale, they start feeling sick." And, like the rookie I was, and like the tobacco I ate, that's exactly what happened to me. Ugh. The next time I ate at Ma Hale's, I was going to take my time.

And the Band Played on

Whenever we drove the cars to games, the infielders always got to travel in the same car. As we continued on to Indiana State, Coach would, as usual, tell us to work on plays while we were driving. Coach wanted us to constantly be ready for anything that could happen during a ball game.

We worked on baseball plays, but when we got tired of it, we transformed ourselves into the Infielder's Band, which we started on the spring trip. Each of us acted like we played an instrument – this ride, I played the sax and clarinet, Itch played the drums, Jerry played the trombone, Dick played the trumpet, and Monty played the bass fiddle. What a combination! I got the band started on our trip to Louisiana.

On another trip, when we were going to play Indiana University, I got the band started. I was just sitting in the back humming when someone turned on the radio. I started be bopping and sang, "Oh, when the Saints, ba ba bomp, come marching in, ba ba bomp, ba bomp, oh when the saints came marching in..."

Then Itch started banging on the steering wheel like he was a drummer, and Jerry played the trombone – "rum bum bum bum." The bass fiddle banged in, and then Dick started blowing on the imaginary trumpet. We thought we were really cool. So whenever a song came on the radio that we really liked, we'd start playing our imaginary instruments.

On this trip, we had about a four-hour drive before lunch. We were having a great time, playing our music in our Infielders Band. Just as on our southern trip, the "St. Louis Blues" came on the radio. We went crazy. We've got our windows rolled down, and everybody is fingering and playing their imaginary instruments. Itch is beating on the steering wheel. We weren't paying attention to anything else, and Itch started pressing down on the gas pedal. Pretty soon, we had gone from being the third car in line to the second car in line. Then we pulled out of the second car position and started to catch up with Coach's car – but on the wrong side of the road. We could see another four or five miles ahead, nobody was coming, but we were just going crazy. As we were playing, all of us looked to the right, and there was Coach driving his car, looking at us playing our imaginary instruments. He didn't say anything, he just kept driving and kept looking at us like we were crazy. Itch slowly pulled his foot off the gas pedal, we faded far behind Coach's car, and pulled back into formation.

We continued to play and be-bop with our Infielders Band. But we made a pact: Never go in front of the second car again.

Why would Coach want to wake the judge?
I'm sure he knew we were going to get fined heavily,
and we might even have to
spend the night in jail. We were mortified.

Hauled Off to Night Court

As the Infield Band played, suddenly the front hood of the second car blew open. It didn't break off, it just blew up and open. Fred was driving, and he pulled over. All the cars behind the second car also pulled over, but Coach, who was in the first car, didn't see what happened. The rest of us got out of the cars and tied the hood down. We took off, but the hood still kept popping up if the car went faster than 30 mph. And, wouldn't you know it? A cop came by, saw what was happening, turned on his siren, and motioned for all of us to pull over. By that time, Coach had double-backed and found us.

"Officer, is there a problem?" he asked.

The police officer apparently noticed the SIU insignia on the sides of our cars.

"Yes sir. Your players can't drive this car."

Looking at the tied down hood, Coach said, "Yeah, that's one problem, but we've also got another problem."

"What's the other problem?"

"Well, we've got to make it to our baseball game tomorrow at Indiana State. We have a ways to go; we're still in Illinois, and now we have this hood problem." I think Coach was trying to get the Illinois police officer to think we were *from* Illinois, hoping that would work in our favor.

114

"Well Coach, I think what you're going to have to do is get some-body out here to get that hood to stay down. In the meantime, the driv-er of this car shouldn't have been driving it," the cop said.

"I'll take complete responsibility," Coach said and turned to us. "Fel-lows, do you think you can drive this car and keep the hood down?" Fred said, "If we keep the speed under 30 miles-per-hour, it won't pop up."

"Then you boys keep it at 30," Coach said.

"If you drive that car, I'm going to give you a ticket." the officer said. "Then, I'm going to have to take you to court, and it's nighttime, so I'm going to have to wake the judge."

"Well, wake him up! Coach said.

We were startled. Why would Coach want to wake the judge? I'm sure he knew we were going to get fined heavily, and we might have to spend the night in jail. But Coach, with his magic touch, had gotten us out of jams in the past. So, we followed the police officer in a caravan into the next town, about 15 miles away.

Coach went into the courthouse for about 45 minutes. When he came out, he was with the judge and the police officer. They all shook hands. Coach got into his car and yelled out to everybody, "Okay, boys, let's go." Everybody wanted to know what happened. We didn't find out until we pulled into Indiana State University.

Another Miracle: No ticket?

When we got there, we gathered around Coach.

"Well boys, I noticed when the judge came into the courtroom, he was wearing a Masonic ring, so I figured he was a Mason. I had my Ma-sonic ring on, so every time he asked me a question, I would raise my right hand to my jaw so he could see my ring. When he was finished asking questions, the judge said, 'Well Officer, I understand why you pulled the coach and his boys over, but I think they've gotta be on their way so they can play that game tomorrow. And,' he added, 'Please don't be too hard on the Indiana State baseball boys, but be sure to beat them.' "

"Did you get a ticket?" we asked Coach.

"No ticket."

"No fine?"

"No fine."

"No penalty?"

"No penalty."

The car hood got fixed during the game the next day, and after taking two out of three from Indiana State, we were on our way back to Carbondale.

When we told Bussie the story, he laughed.

"Only Coach could have gotten you out of that jam," he told us.

The guard told Bussie he would have to
stay with the bus
until the game was over.
'If you don't, someone might think
you were a prisoner.
And you certainly wouldn't want
to stay here overnight.'

Jailbirds

We successfully escaped going to jail in our last escapade, but on our next adventure, we did find ourselves in jail. About the middle of the season, I noticed that we were scheduled to play a ballgame at Menard

State Prison. I asked Itch about the game. Every other year he said, the team traveled to Chester, Illinois, where the prison was. He said it was always a lot of fun. Sounded fun to me too, if a little spooky.

The day came. We all took our uniform bags packed with our gear and headed off to Chester, with Bussie at the wheel for the hour-long ride. At the prison, Bussie pulled in through two large gates that opened automatically, just for us, I guessed. A prison guard waiting for us said to follow him. He also told Bussie he would have to stay with the bus until the game was over. "If you don't, someone might think you were a prisoner. You certainly wouldn't want to stay here overnight," he said, and Bussie agreed. He would just stay in the bus and read.

We followed the guard into the large prison building and into a waiting room with a wired door in the middle of the room that was flanked by steel-framed wire that ran from one wall to the other. The guard talked through a walkie-talkie to someone on the other side of the wired door, which then clicked open. After we had all passed through, the door automatically closed with a loud slam and then a click. We were in prison now for sure.

The guard took us to what he called the "dressing room," which was nothing but another large room. We left our dress clothes on long tables, put on our uniforms, and followed the guard again. We went through another heavy door and down a long hall. Except for our footsteps, it was real quiet, and kind of eerie. We were carrying our gloves, spikes, and the bases and four of the guys carried the ball bags, too. We went through another large door with a "No Exit" sign, and found ourselves standing in the middle of the prison yard. After being inside the dark building, the sun was so bright we couldn't see at first, but our eyes adjusted, and then we saw prisoners everywhere. They were lifting

117

weights, shooting baskets, throwing horseshoes, and playing checkers, chess, and cards.

I wondered where the ball field was until another guard blew a whistle and yelled, "CLEAR THE COURT. IF YOU WANT TO WATCH THE GAME, HELP PULL UP THE BENCHES."

Makeshift Field

So, this was it – the "playing field," with cinder blocks for "grass" under our feet. We had the bases with us so we made up a ball field. Right field was the wall. Left field went forever and ever. There were no lines between home plate and first base, or home plate and third base, so I asked if I could measure the baselines. One of the guards asked, "Do you have the powder?" I said, "Yes, I do!" We didn't have any string to make a straight line between home and first, or home and third, so I just dropped the powder where I thought the baseline would be.

Two umpires strolled over to us and asked us if we were ready to play. We hadn't even warmed up yet, but Coach said, "We're ready!" The prisoners took the field first. We watched them throw the ball around the infield and take some ground balls. They looked good. The first baseman was huge and had hands bigger than baseball gloves. The outfielders were throwing long fly balls to each other. They looked like they had good arms.

I was the lead-off man. On the first pitch, I hit a single over second base to the
center fielder. I rounded first and then came back to the base.

"Hey man, good hit!" the big first baseman said. "I'm glad you guys came. We haven't had a game yet this year." I was surprised; they looked like they had played a lot.

"Looks like you practice a fair amount," I said.

"Every day we can practice and get out of that cell, we do."

Our team got one hit after another, and were winning 7-0, before the prison team came up to bat. The first guy hit a single, the second guy walked. The third guy, who was the first baseman, hit a ball so far over our left-fielder's head that he didn't even have to run around the bases.

Now they had three runs to our seven. They made three outs, and we came up to bat again. The next time I was up, I hit another single to centerfield. I rounded first base, came back to the base. Again, the first baseman said, "Hey! Nice hit!"

"Hey, how about yours? That ball was hit hard and long," I said.

"Yeah, I wish I was out of here," he said. "I think I could play for some professional team."

A Grisly Crime

We got two more runs; I scored one of them. Then, we were out in the field again. Before I went out, I walked over to the officer who was standing next to our bench and asked, "Hey, what's the first baseman in prison for?" The officer looked at me. "He strangled his wife – he's here for a long time."

I thought about those big hands and felt a cold shiver. I didn't say much to him after that.

Dick, our first baseman, came up to bat and hit one over the wall. That wall was about 30 feet high and about 310 feet away. The inmates sitting in the stands stood up and chanted, "Warden, Warden, can I go get it?" Everybody in the yard was yelling the same thing. We laughed along with them.

His next time up, the first baseman hit a line shot up against the wall, five feet from the top. He got a triple. I got another single. As I was coming back to first base, he said, "Man, you're hot – three for three! All singles!"

"Yeah, but I didn't hit them far, like you do. You've hit two big blasts."

Wishful thinking

"Yeah, I wish I was out of here. I really think I could play for some professional team," he said again. On the next pitch, I stole second base. I didn't talk to him anymore.

Soon, the game was over. We won 14-5. Then it was time to shower. It was a huge shower — all metal with about 30 shower heads. We got dressed, packed our uniforms and gear, and then headed down the halls behind the guard. He said we were going to the mess hall. All the time, door locks were clicking open in front of us and clicking closed behind us. The inmates shuffled back to their cells.

Bussie joined us, and we ate by ourselves. There were no prisoners. You name it, we had it – mashed potatoes, gravy, corn on the cob, salad, meatloaf, bread, butter, lemonade, and dessert was cherry pie. As we walked out of the building to the bus, we could hear the big doors still clicking and banging shut in front of and behind us.

We asked Bussie what he did while we were playing ball. "I just stayed in the bus and read. I thought about walking around, but then I kept seeing those prison guards in their towers. It was weird. So, I stayed in the bus."

On the ride back to Carbondale, the guys were talking about the big first baseman. Dick asked me what we were talking about when I was on first. I said "We were congratulating each other on our hits. He said that he wished he was out of there because he thought he could play for a professional team. As a matter of fact, he told me that twice. That's when I stole second and got out of there." Itch then asked if I knew what he was in for. I said, "Yeah. He strangled his wife with those big hands."

Dick looked stricken. We were quiet the rest of the way back.

CHAPTER SEVENTEEN

Breaking League Records

I walked inside, and a co-ed was
playing pool by herself.
She told me her name was Rose.

A Co-Ed Stops Time

Not long after we were in "jail," we traveled to Northern Illinois University, in DeKalb. Their baseball team was in second place, three games behind us. Only two weekends of conference games were left. If they swept all three games, we would be tied for first place. We didn't know how Western Illinois was doing, but they were close too. We couldn't let Northern take all three games and be tied with us for first place. We had to beat them.

Bussie pulled us into the Northern Illinois University campus dorm just before suppertime. Some of our ballplayers went out after dinner, but I decided to stay in the dorm and relax that night. I knew our curfew was 10 p.m., and it was about 8 p.m. when I was walking to our assigned sleeping area.

I noticed a game room off to the left side of the hallway with a couple of ping-pong tables and a pool table.

I walked inside, and there was a co-ed playing pool by herself. She told me her name was Rose. I introduced myself and told her that I played on the Southern Illinois baseball team that was playing against Northern, her school, the next day and Saturday. I looked around, and she said, "Hey! You wanna play pool?"

"Sure."

After we had played awhile, I looked down at my watch and it was 9:15 p.m. I still had 45 minutes. Just then, Coach came by and said, "Hardy, don't forget curfew is 10:00."

"Yes, sir! I'm not leaving the building. I'll be there; I've got plenty of time." He walked on. So, we played about another 15 or 20 minutes, and Rose said, "Aren't you concerned about curfew?"

"Nah. It's probably only about 9:30."

"I've got 10:10," she said. I looked at my watch again and it still showed 9:15. Whoops. I was in trouble.

We had to win at least one
of the two games on Saturday
to tie for the conference championship.

I quickly told Rose good-bye and ran down to the visitors lounge and sleeping area where all of my teammates were all in their rooms and in their beds, except me. I immediately heard Coach's voice.

"You're late!"

"Coach, when I saw you, my watch said 9:15." I showed him that it still said 9:15 p.m.

"Well son, you've got to be smarter than your watch. You've got to know when curfew is." That was all he said, but the next day, I didn't start the first game.

Around the fourth inning, Coach asked, "Do you think it is the right TIME for you to play?"

"Yes, sir!"

"Okay, go take a lap down there towards that big oak tree." Well, that oak tree was about a half a mile away, so I ran down and around that tree as fast as I could.

When I came back, we had runners on both second and third bases with two outs, Coach put me in to hit. I didn't know if I was just pinch hitting, or if I was going to stay in the game and play. I didn't care right then, I just wanted to get in the game and get a base hit.

The first pitch was as big as a grapefruit and as slow as a Satchel Paige change-up. I hit it as hard as I could. It went out to right center, and by the time the right fielder threw it back to the second baseman, I was standing on second base. I played the entire rest of the game, going three for three.

We won that game 5-1 and split the double-header, winning the early game 6-4, and losing the night game 3-4. From then on, I didn't trust my watch. I always asked someone else what time it was to make sure I was never late for curfew again. But other guys pushed the limits.

A.W.O.L!

The next week, we traveled to Illinois State in Normal, Illinois. We blew them away the first game, 9-1. We only had to take one game to be conference champions. The night we won, I was in our quarters by 9 p.m. Around 9:45 p.m. Coach came in and said, "Is everybody here?" We all looked around. Three guys, Mel, Fred and Dick – all starters, our best hitters, first baseman, right fielder, and our center fielder, weren't in yet. They were A.W.O.L. But no one said a word.

"Nobody's telling me whether everybody's in or not, so I'm going to wait in the lobby upstairs until about 10:30, and then I'll come back and do room check," Coach said.

No one knew what to do, but I had an idea to help the guys circumvent Coach.

I went upstairs to the lobby.

If we swept them and won all three,
we would be the 1959 IIAC
Champions. SIU would be on top–#1.

"What are you doing out here, Hardy?" Coach asked.

"Coach, it's still a couple minutes until 10, and I wanted to come up and see if they had any books or a magazine I can take back and read for a couple of minutes." Just then, I saw Mel, Fred, and Dick walking towards the big glass front door of the building. Not wanting them to get caught, I grabbed a magazine and yelled, "Hey Coach! Come here a minute. Let me show you something. Look at this."

Coach walked over to me with his back to the front door. As he looked down at the magazine, I motioned behind him for the guys to come in. A second later, they disappeared. I didn't know where they were, but I figured they had enough time to get back in the building, into our room, and in bed.

Coach said, "I don't understand what you are showing me."

"The story on this page is really interesting!" I closed the magazine, put it back in the rack, and took off back to the room, leaving Coach scratching his head.

As I bolted, I heard Coach say, "I'm going to take one more look outside, and then I'll be back to the room to make sure everybody's in."

I went back in, and sure enough, the three guys had gotten in. Dick yelled out, "Hey Hardy! Thanks!" The other two guys gave me the high sign. They said they got in by climbing up some vines and banging on the window.

Just then, Coach came in, looked around, counted, and saw everybody was there and said, "Okay boys, good-night."

Phew!

The Final Game

We were now down to the final weekend of playoffs in the conference. For the last month of the season, we were watching Northern Illinois and Western Illinois to see how close to us they were in the standings. It turned out both teams were swept by Central Illinois two weeks in a row. The first week, Northern Illinois lost all three games to Central; the next week, Western lost all three games to Central. We lost one game each, and now found ourselves coming into the final weekend playing Central. We were trailing them by one game. We had been in first place all throughout the season, and now we found ourselves in second place. We were scheduled to play a single game with Central Friday and a double-header on Saturday at Carbondale, which most students referred to as "Southern." We had to win Friday's game to go into Saturday tied for first place. We had to win at least one of the two games on Saturday to tie for the conference championship. If we swept them and won all three, then we would be the 1959 Illinois Inter-Collegiate Athletic Conference Champions. Southern would be on top – Number 1.

A Fond Look Back

Friday, the day of the first game against Central Illinois, as I got dressed in the locker room, I thought back over the season. March, April, May, and the first week of June had come and gone so quickly. The Animals, Woody Hall, eating with the girls, the holes in the wall (poor Dave, he owed the school about 250 bucks), my 624 roommate, Pod, across the hall, the geese, the ducks, the ladies, the drunks, Vic, with his shotgun, WOMB, the Menard State prison, making shortstop on the team the first year, going into the series hitting over 330 (basically one hit for every three times at bat), — Wow! What an exciting three-and-a-half months. Now, I was ready for the last stretch!

I put on my uniform and jogged out to the ball field. Running past the fountain, I threw in a penny I had saved for the occasion – the wish was to win 'em all. Bring out the broom, do the sweep. I looked at the boy and girl under the umbrella. They looked back at me, and I swear they both smiled. I smiled back, gave them the high-five sign and started towards the ball field. I was the first one to arrive at the park, so I unlocked the barn, got the bats, balls, bases, and lime bucket, and started my work. As I lined the field, players on both teams arrived. They were all warming up on different parts of the ball field. We took infield practice first, throwing the ball around the horn, first playing catch. Then the infielders and outfielders played pepper.

Itch and I didn't know it then,
but we had broken a league record for double plays
between a shortstop and second baseman
in the IIAC.

Pepper was a great game. Usually three to five fielders stand about 30 feet away from the batter. One at a time, the fielders throw the ball to the batter. The batter just hits the ball back to the fielder, one at a time, not hard, but firmly, to try to get good bat control, back and forth, back and forth. Then, one of the players with a glove changes with the person who has the bat, and it keeps rotating. Pepper really gives the batter great batting control and hones the fielders' reactions.

Game Time!

They went down one, two, three in the first inning,
but we did too.

Tuck was the starting pitcher, as he had been all season for Friday games. His record was now nine and one. The opposing pitcher was a right-hander, who, from watching him down the left field line in the bullpen, looked to be throwing bullets.

The coach called us together. "Now boys, I don't have to tell you how important this series is, but let's start it off right by taking this first game. Tuck, how do you feel?"

"Good Coach!"

"How do you boys feel?"

"GREAT, COACH!" we shouted.

"All right, take the field."

Tuck took his warm-up pitches, and we took our infield and ground balls from Dick over at first base. The outfielders threw long fly balls to each other.

129

Then the umpire, the Man in Blue, shouted "PLAY BALL!"

They went down one-two-three in the first inning, but we did too. The opposing, right-handed pitcher was throwing bullets. He threw me five pitches. I think I saw two of them, and then I heard the umpire yell, "STRIKE THREE!"

The second inning was the same – no hits, no runs, no errors for either team. In the third inning, Central Illinois' second batter, a left-handed batter, bunted down the third baseline and beat it out for a single. So they had one out and a man on first. I came in from shortstop to talk to Tuck. "Okay now Tuck, if he bunts, we'll let you know where to throw, either to first or second base."

"Okay, Hardy. Just let me know."

The first batter had already struck out, so there was one out and one on. On the first pitch, the next batter faked a bunt. He turned around to bunt, and then, at the last minute, he pulled his bat back and hit a hard ground ball to the left of Itch at second base. Itch got it on the second bounce, rotated back around toward the infield, and threw to me coming across second base. I tagged the base this time with my trailing right foot, pivoted, and threw right at the head of the oncoming runner, who got down and out of the way immediately. I had thrown a strike to the first baseman. The umpire called, "OUT!" at second base. The umpire called, "OUT" at first base. We were out of the inning with one hit, no runs, no errors, and one double play.

That was the 17th double play of the season. Itch and I didn't know it then, but we had broken a league record for double plays between a shortstop and second baseman in the IIAC.

In our half of the inning, we went down one-two-three again. During the next inning, they got their first two men on base on sharp singles to right field, with both batters being right-handed. This meant they were hitting behind Tuck's fastball. He was throwing the ball past them pretty often, but they were still getting a piece of it and hitting to right field. I went in from shortstop again to talk to Tuck.

"Tuck, what's going on?"

"They're hitting my good fastball."

"What about your curveball?"

"I haven't thrown it yet."

Dead Man's Curveball

"Well, now might be a good time to throw it, but here's the deal, there's two on and no outs – the perfect time to bunt. We'll let you know where to throw the ball."

The next batter up also was a right-handed hitter. Tuck went into his stretch, looked at the runner on second base, looked at the runner on first, and threw the curveball. The batter bunted. He bunted it down the third baseline. Tuck ran over to get it, but it was a perfect bunt, hugging the baseline. By the time he got to it, there was no play at third or at second, so we waved him off. "FIRST BASE! FIRST BASE! FIRST BASE!" I called. He whirled and threw it. The runner was out, with men on second and third. Tuck walked the next batter.

Now the game got interesting. The bases were loaded, with one out, the game tied at zero each. The next batter had two balls and two strikes on him when Tuck threw a curveball. Because Tuck is left-handed, the curveball went away from the left-handed batter towards the outside of the plate, on the third base side. The batter hit a shot, one bounce just to my right. I backhanded it with my glove, pivoted back with my right foot, and fired over to Itch, who was some-how standing right on top of second base. Itch was quick. He always seemed to know where the ball was going. With one foot on each side of the base, he tagged the bag with his left foot, rotated, and threw to first base. The umpired called, "OUT" at second base and "OUT" at first base. We were out of the inning again with two hits, no runs, no errors, and another double play. How much more fun could we have? How much more exciting could it get? But now, we had to get some runs. The score was still tied 0-0.

A Good Bunt: 'Sometimes the Ball Just has Eyes.'

The game went into the seventh inning with no score. Central Illinois went down one-two-three with Tuck still pitching great. Tuck was the first man up. I was the lead-off man, so I was up at bat after Tuck. The first pitch hit Tuck in the right shoulder. That was certainly something the pitcher did not want to do, hit a batter, especially the opposing pitcher, in the seventh inning, with a tied ballgame of 0-0.

I came up to bat and looked down the third baseline. The coach was giving me a bunt signal. It was skin to skin, hand across the chest, no rub off – definitely a bunt. Tuck was on first. On the first pitch, I squared around to bunt, but it was low. In fact, it went into the dirt, and all the way back to the backstop. Tuck went to second base.

Now, we've got a man on second and my count is one ball, no strikes. I looked down to the coach's box – skin to skin, a hand across the chest–the bunt sign is still on. I figured I could bunt the ball down the third baseline, and the third baseman would have to come in to get it to throw me out. If he came in to get it and didn't go back to third base after he made the play, there was a good possibility Tuck could have made it to third. The shortstop is supposed to cover third base on this type of play, but it was a long way for the shortstop to come. In the meantime, Tuck, on second base, knew I was going to bunt, so he took a little bit longer lead off second base. If I could lay it down (bunt it on the ground), Tuck would take off for third base.

The next pitch came in, and I squared around to bunt, taking another ball outside. I looked down at the coach – skin to skin, across the chest, then a rub off on the arms – no bunt. Wait a minute! He changed the sign. Now, it's skin to skin, across the chest again and nothing after that. He then walked forward and said, "Come on, Hardy! Get a hit!" The bunt was on. Two balls, no strikes. The pitcher had to come to home plate with a strike this time or walk me if he threw another ball. He threw a ball right down the middle of the plate. I squared around and bunted it.

The ball had gone over the center fielder's head.
Tuck took off and scored. I scored.
Itch was on my heels, scoring
about five steps behind me.

The ball went down the third baseline, hugging the line. The third baseman came in. The catcher yelled, "LET IT GO! LET IT GO! IT WILL ROLL FOUL." The whole time, I'm running to first base and Tuck is running to third. The ball was still rolling right down the line I put down about an hour before the ballgame started. It rolled and rolled. The catcher was looking. The pitcher was looking. The third baseman was looking. As I was hitting first base, I turned my head to see what was going on. I rounded first base and took off for second. No infielders saw me running towards second. They were still watching the ball roll. The ball continued to roll as I ran to second. Tuck was already standing on third base. The ball was still rolling – right down the line into the third base bag for a base hit, a double at that. Sometimes it's not how far or hard you hit 'em, but where you hit 'em. Sometimes, the ball just has eyes. This time it did.

So Tuck was at third, and I was on second. Itch was up. We looked to the coach to see the signal to hit away, but the pitcher and catcher were meeting. They decided to load the bases, and then walked Itch intentionally with four straight pitches. Four called balls, and Itch went to first.

We had bases loaded and no outs with Dick up to bat. Dick was one of our most powerful home run hitters on the team. We looked to the coach for the signal. Instead, he yelled, "DICK, HIT AWAY!"

And So He Did...

On the very first pitch, Dick hit a shot that kept going. The coach yelled, "TAG UP! TAG UP!" We tagged up. The ball was flying out to the outfield, and the left fielder and center fielder were running at each other. Then, I noticed they turned to go deep. The ball went over the center fielder's head. Tuck took off and scored. I scored. Itch was on my heels, scoring about five steps behind me. Dick ended up on third base with a three-RBI triple.

We were winning 3-0. The next batter, our center fielder, hit a long, towering fly ball, but their center fielder caught it. Dick tagged and scored easily from third base. We then made another two outs, closing out the inning. We were winning 4-0 with two innings to go.

Tuck pitched the eighth and ninth innings and kept Illinois Central from scoring. We didn't get any hits either, and the game ended, 4-0. We won and were now tied for first place with Central Illinois, who we'd just beaten for the first of three games. Saturday – it all came down to Saturday, the next day. We needed to win both games to nab the IIAC Baseball Championship. That was our plan – win two.

We thought we had a great crowd at the Friday game, but when I arrived early at the ballpark on Saturday to put down the lines and the bases, there was already a crowd forming. "Come on, Hardy! Get that field in good shape. Let's make sure we win two today," people in the crowd shouted.

I yelled back at them: "WIN TWO! WIN TWO! THAT'S WHAT WE WANNA DO! WIN TWO! WIN TWO! THAT'S WHAT WE WANNA DO!"

Catch and Pepper

'WHY DON'T YOU TAKE
THOSE WEIGHTS OFF YOUR FEET
SO YOU CAN START RUNNING FAST?'

By now, both teams were on the field warming up, stretching, playing catch and pepper. Immediately the Illinois Central players started heckling us.

"HEY YOU! SALUKIS! WHAT IS A SALUKI? IT'S A DUMB-LOOKING DOG! JUST LIKE YOU ARE! WE'RE GONNA BEAT YOU GUYS BAD TODAY!"

They were yelling and screaming.

Well, we had a great heckler on our team too – Harley. He would yell things like, "HEY MAN! YOUR FACE IS SO RED, YOU'RE

ABOUT TO BLOW A GASKET!" or "HEY RUNNER! WHY DON'T YOU TAKE THOSE WEIGHTS OFF YOUR FEET SO YOU CAN START RUNNING FAST?" He'd rip everybody. Now seemed like the right time, because the other team was riding us pretty heavy, but we also had other hecklers: Dave, Jerry, and Gene – The Animals.

He walked real slow and his side-to side gait
was almost like an elephant's –
boom, boom, boom, boom.

They didn't need to do much heckling the first game as it went by quickly. It was a blur, but we won. It seemed like everything went our way. If we hit a pop-up, it fell for a base hit. If we hit a ground ball, it went where nobody was. We didn't hit any atom balls. Atom balls are when you hit it hard, but you hit it right at somebody. No atom balls in the first game; we found holes everywhere, and it was an easy win, 11-3.

Now we were one game up going into the second Saturday game, which was the last game of the season in the conference. If we won, we were the conference champions. If we lost, we were tied for conference, and we would have to play another game Monday.

Coach called us all together. "I have one question for you. Do you guys want to play after this?"

"NO, SIR!" everybody yelled.

"Then, there's only one thing to do, boys. And that is win this game right now. Let's be a team. Play within yourselves. If everybody plays their positions correctly, we'll win."

Central had a left-handed starting pitcher, who must have also played football. He was not only big, at least 250 pounds, but he also looked really mean. He looked like he was out of shape because he had a big belly. He walked real slow, and his side-to side gait was almost like an elephant's – boom, boom, boom, boom.

From the beginning of the game, The Animals were all over him. Dave, Gene, and Jerry were sitting at the beginning of the first row, closest to home plate. Whenever he took a step, the trio would yell out, "Boom! Boom! Boom! Boom!" After taking batting practice and having the trio "Boom" him to death, he turned around, looked at them, and kept looking at them as he slowly walked away. That's when Dave yelled out, "YEAH! LOOK OVER HERE, BIG BOY. I'M GONNA EAT YOU FOR A SNACK! I'M GONNA KILL YOU. WHEN THIS GAME'S OVER, I'M GOING TO BREAK YOU INTO LITTLE PIECES! I'LL PUT YOU IN A LITTLE MATCHBOX AND WE'LL SHIP YOU BACK HOME!"

The trio rode him the whole game. They would stand up, bounce from one leg to another, and would either chant at him or yell "BOOM! BOOM! BOOM! BOOM!" and pat their bellies.

But Central scored three runs in the second inning like it was nothing.

On three straight pitches, our batters hit
a triple, a double, and a single
to put us in the lead 6-5.
Then, we went down one-two-three.

The first two men came up and hit shots to the outfield, one over Itch's head at second base and one over my head at shortstop. The next batter came up and hit a triple, scoring the first two runs. The next man hit a deep fly ball to center field, which we caught, but their runner on third base was practically able to walk home with the third run.

They were winning 3-0, going into the third inning. Then they got two more runs in the third inning by hitting a home run with a runner on second. The ball busted out a car window in the left field parking lot. They were winning 5-0, and we went down one-two-three in the third. Thank goodness they went down one, two, three in the bottom of the fourth. Now we were coming up to bat in the top of the fourth, trailing 5-0.

The whole time, Harley, our guy who always rode and razzed the other team, was doing everything he could to get their ears. He was calling them skinny bean heads, whatever came into his mind. The Animals were all over the opposing team's left-handed pitcher, the elephant-walker, with their cheers and chants. Every time he moved a step or took a stride, they would give him the "Boom! Boom! Boom! Boom!" The problem was it didn't seem to rattle him.

Then, in the bottom of the fourth, we got a run. Dick hit one so far over the right fielder's head that by the time he got the ball (there was no fence in our ballpark), Dick had already rounded third base. There was no way to get him at home so he walked along the baseline and stepped on home plate for our first run.

Time to Load Up the Bases

Now, the score was 5-1 going into the fifth inning. They went down one-two-three again. We scored three runs. Our left fielder, Tony, hit a double between the left and center fielders. Then, our catcher, J.W., hit a little dying swan that fell over their shortstop's head into deep short, too far out for the shortstop, and too shallow for the left fielder to get. Tony held at second, making sure the ball wasn't caught. We had base runners on first and second with no outs.

Then, Tuck came up to bat and walked. The bases were loaded. The opposing elephant pitcher thought he threw a strike on the last pitch to Tuck. He got really upset and just stared at the home plate umpire, who had called it a ball. Well, that was all the trio needed. They gave him a new name.

"HEY DUMBO! WHY DON'T YOU THROW IT UP WITH YOUR TRUNK INSTEAD OF YOUR HAND?" Dave shouted.

It still didn't seem to bother the pitcher. He just got ready to throw again, which he did. I was up. I looked down the third baseline to Coach. Was there a signal on? He went through the motions, gave the bunt sign, rubbed his cheek for skin-to-skin, and then yelled out, "OKAY HARDY, YOU'RE HITTING AWAY," which was the indicator for a squeeze bunt. That meant Tony, on third, was going to break home as soon as their pitcher threw the ball. My first job was to make sure I didn't miss the ball so their catcher would catch it, and Tony would be an easy out at home plate. My second job was to bunt the ball fair, and I squeeze bunted down the third baseline. The third baseman had no idea the bunt was coming. He charged the ball, but by the time he got to it, Tony had already slid across home plate, and I was already running across first base for a squeeze bunt base hit RBI.

Then, none of us on base saw the signal, but their pitcher, looking at home plate, suddenly stepped off the rubber, whirled, and threw to the third baseman, who was moving back towards third. Tuck was leaning towards home, and when he dove back to third, the umpire raised his right hand and yelled, "OUT!" There was no doubt about it, he was out. The crowd went quiet.

Then our right fielder hit a rocket over the left fielder's head, and the ball went into the parking lot. Fair ball – home run. Three runs – now we were losing 5-4. That was all for us in the fifth as the next two batters grounded out to their third baseman, who threw perfect strikes to their first baseman.

Double-Header: 'We Were Losing'

We went into the sixth inning. In our conference, when you played a double-header, each game was only seven innings. We had to hold them for the next two innings and get a least one run to tie, or two or more runs to get ahead.

At the top of the sixth, they got a runner on second, but Jerry made a great play on a ball the batter bounced high off home plate down the third baseline. At first, it looked like the batter was going to beat it out, but Jerry came in, picked up the ball bare-handed on the second bounce, and threw the ball from where he caught it, beating the runner by a half a step. That was the third out.

We were losing 5-4 and came up to bat in the bottom of the sixth. On three straight pitches, our batters hit a triple, a double, and a single to put us in the lead 6-5. Then we went down one-two-three. The Animals began their rant, "DUMBO! DUMBO! DUMBO!" The inning went by quickly – three pitches, three hits, two runs, and three outs, and we're back in the field. Just before the outs, the craziest thing happened. At first, it had seemed that The Animals' ranting wasn't bothering the elephant pitcher, but I guess it was because he went into his stretch and stopped right there.

The ball just seemed to be hanging up in the air.
It seemed like an eternity until it started coming down.
And when it did, it was too late.

140

In the 'Yeah, Right' Category

Dumbo was left-handed, so in his stretch position, he was looking right at the trio. He wound up, and instead of throwing the ball towards home plate, he threw the ball into the stands where the trio were sitting. He didn't hit them because he was a little short with his throw, but the umpire called it a ball and ran out to the pitcher's mound.

I could hear him from home plate asking the pitcher, "What are you doing?"

"I lost control of the ball," the pitcher said.

In the meantime, Dave had the ball. The umpire said, "Throw the ball back in."

"Tell the pitcher to come over and get it," Dave said. The umpire grabbed another ball and threw it out to the pitcher.

Special Guests in the Stands

Finally, we were in the seventh inning – the last inning of the season, and we hoped we wouldn't have to bat again. If we won, we would be the conference champions. The crowd was going crazy.

My mom, dad, and Tom had come to the game, and they stood up, yelling and cheering. It was the first time I saw them the whole day. At least 500 people were yelling and jumping up and down in the stands and along the sidelines. Horns were honking in the street and in the parking lots. People gathered along the third baseline and behind the backstop. Of all people, I even saw Dr. Rainbow, my English teacher. Our wrestling coach and football coach were there, along with their staff.

Jim had pitched a good game so far. He allowed five runs but was still throwing hard. The first batter was Dumbo. The Animals were standing about 30 feet from him, yelling and screaming at him, but it didn't seem to bother him this time. On Jim's first pitch, the batter hit a shot over Itch's head, into right field for a single. He hit the ball so hard that the right fielder almost had time to throw him out at first base.

The next batter tried to bunt the first two pitches, but the balls ran foul. The batter had two strikes against him, with no outs, and a man on first base. Their coach must have called the bunt off because on the next pitch, the batter lined one over my head for a single.

'It's not how fast and straight you throw,
it's how fast and how much movement
you have on the ball,' I said.

Runners were on first and second bases, no outs. We were winning, 6-5, but if they tied the score or got another run, and we didn't score in the bottom part of the inning, we would lose. A lot was at stake.

"TIME OUT!" Coach yelled from the bench. Coach talked to Jim and then motioned down the line to the bullpen to bring Tuck in. Tuck had pitched nine innings the day before.

"You think Tuck's got anything left?" Itch asked Coach.

"All we need are a couple of pitches," Coach said.

Tuck walked onto the field. Before he started throwing his warm-up pitches, I asked him how he felt.

"I feel good. I don't even feel like I pitched yesterday. My arm feels strong. I hope the ball's moving." He threw his first practice pitch, and after catching the ball coming back from J.W, he said to me, "And the ball's moving."

"That's what we want," I said, "It's not how fast and straight you

142

throw, it's how fast and how much movement you have on the ball."

"Fast with movement. That's what they're going to get today," Tuck said.

So nobody was out, and men were on first and second. Their next batter already had two hits and two RBIs in the game. The Animals were still yelling at Dumbo who was now on second base.

A Swing and a Miss

The next batter swung at the first pitch and missed. On the next pitch, he hit a ball that bounced off home plate, straight up in the air. It looked like it went up in the clouds, and Tuck was waiting for it to come down. Dumbo was waddling towards third base. The man on first base was running to second. The batter is sprinting to first. The ball just seems to be hanging up in the air. It seemed like an eternity until it started to come down. When it did, it was too late. By the time it came down and Tuck grabbed it, whirled, and threw, the runner had already crossed first base.

The crowd was quiet. No one on our team said a thing. The opposing team was yelling and screaming. They knew we were in trouble. They were losing 6-5, but they had the bases loaded, men on first, second, and third, nobody out, and their best batter was up to bat.

Tuck walked around the mound, bent over to grab the rosin bag behind the pitcher's rubber, adjusted his hat, tugged at his pants with his left throwing arm, grabbed his left ear, and looked towards home plate.

"Tuck, just throw strikes!" I yelled. The crowd was still quiet. Tuck wound up, threw a ball in the dirt in front of home plate, but somehow J.W. stopped the ball from going back to the backstop. He fell right on top of the ball and smothered it with his glove on the left side of home plate. That was close! A wild pitch and Dumbo on third might have scored.

The next pitch, Tuck threw a curveball that didn't curve. It didn't do anything. It just hung outside and was called a ball.

Central's players were yelling and screaming, pulling for their hitter, yelling,

"Get a hit! Hit a grand slammer – anything! Just make contact with the ball! You can do it. Wait for your pitch! Hit it out of here!"

The Animal trio was quiet, and our fans weren't making a sound. They were all watching Tuck as he wound up and threw the ball down the middle of the plate. The batter took a ferocious swing and missed. J. W. threw the ball back to Tuck and yelled, "Tuck, that's the way to throw the ball!" Tuck went to the back of the mound, pulled down the bill of his cap, looked out at me, and gave me a big smile.

"Thank goodness he feels good," I thought. I gave him a big smile back and yelled, "One more strike, Tuck! One more strike!"

Tuck got his signal from J.W. for a curveball. He nodded and threw a good one. The batter looked like he knew the curveball was coming. He took a hard swing and hit a long fly ball down the left field line. If it had stayed fair, it could have easily been a sacrifice fly, and Dumbo on third base would tag up and score. But, at the last second, it went foul just before it rolled onto the parking lot.

Dumbo was just touching home plate when he heard
the umpire at second base yell,
'OUT!'

Two strikes, two balls, bases loaded, the best hitter on their team was up, and the best pitcher on our team was pitching. Tuck got the signal:

A fastball. He walked around the mound, stretched down, and touched his shoe tops, grabbed his left earlobe, and clutched his right shoulder with his left hand. He turned and looked at each one of the infielders, who were all yelling, "Okay Tuck! You can do it! Throw a strike! Put some heat on it! Make that ball move! Throw it down the middle!"

The next pitch was a fastball. The batter started to swing but held back – the ball was just above the letters of his uniform. The umpire called a ball, the third one.

J.W., Itch, and I walked out to the mound. J.W. spoke up.

"Tuck, you gotta throw a strike now. This is it! This is what you've been waiting for the whole year. We're going to win this game. You throw it over; we'll win the game."

"We're behind you, Tuck," I said.

"Okay guys, I'm throwing a strike," Tuck said.

It seemed like everything happened in slow motion. Tuck started his wind-up and threw a fastball that looked like it was going to take a slow 15 seconds to get to home plate. The ball looked bright white, big and hittable. Whatever happened, this wasn't going to be Ball Four. The batter saw the ball coming, he cocked his bat, swung, and hit a shot straight ahead. It was going so fast, Tuck didn't even see it until the last second. He threw his gloved hand up to stop it, but the ball hit the heel of his glove with so much force the glove almost came off his hand.

Elephant Walk

The ball arced and hurtled forward into centerfield. My first instinct was to break to my left towards second base, where the ball was headed. The runner on second took off towards third as I ran out to short centerfield. Out of the corner of my right eye, I could see the man on first running to second. At the same time, Dumbo was doing an elephant walk from third to home plate. He smiled at J.W., our catcher, and stuck his tongue out like a third-grader. While Dumbo waddled towards home plate with the tying run, I ran as hard as I could, watching the ball in the air as it moved toward centerfield. I was still running hard, and I could finally see the ball start to come down in its arc. If it landed on the ground, they were going to get at least two runs. I couldn't let that happen – I had to catch the ball.

The ball started to fall toward the ground, deep behind second base. I was still running full speed and watching nothing but the ball. I took my last step, timed my dive, and dove forward with my left gloved hand extended. I was flying and floating through the air with my glove arm extended out as far as it would go. Things were still moving in slow motion as the ball fell right into my open glove just before I hit the ground. I put my right hand over the glove, covering the ball. I hit the ground with such force that I bounced up and rolled over twice, but I held onto the ball. I was dazed and everything went black for a second.

I heard footsteps and people yelling, and when I opened my eyes, I saw only a blur. Where is everyone? I started to panic. I couldn't see where to throw the ball, so I closed my eyes tight for one millisecond, and when I opened them, the blur was gone, and I saw everything clearly.

"Throw to third! Throw to third!" Itch was yelling. Dumbo was just touching home plate when he heard the umpire at second base yell, "OUT!"

"Okay, fat boy, let's see you get back to third base!" J.W. yelled. They were both facing each other at home plate.

J.W., with a big wad of Beechnut chew in his mouth and a snarl on his face, began ribbing Dumbo, who, with a blank stare, turned back toward third base but slipped and fell on his knees. As he was getting up, the trio started yelling and screaming at him:

"HEY DUMBO! YOU THINK YOU CAN MAKE IT BACK TO THIRD BASE TODAY?" Dumbo knew he had to get back before I threw the ball to Jerry at third base.

In spite of my catching the ball, hitting the ground, bouncing up, doing a somersault, then a roll, I actually had plenty of time to throw to any base. Between Itch and J.W. telling me where to throw, I got my bearings, planted my back foot, and threw to Jerry at third base. Dumbo wasn't even halfway back to third. He was waddling as fast as he could, but he couldn't make it. He sank to his knees and pounded the ground. The umpire behind home plate yelled, "THE RUNNER IS OUT!"

While all this was going on, the SIU crowd was going crazy, cheering, yelling, screaming, and jumping up and down. The trio was doing a cheer, "GO SOUTHERN GO! GO SOUTHERN GO!" I had thrown a perfect strike to Jerry at third base. While I made the throw, Itch ran back to cover second base. The runner on second, who was heading to third, had stopped after hearing the umpire yell, "Out!" and was on his way back to second base. After stepping on third, Jerry was ready to throw to second, but Itch wasn't back to second base yet. Jerry knew there were two outs already and he decided to throw the ball to Dick at first base. He threw a perfect strike. The runner was only halfway back to first base when Dick caught the ball. The Man in Blue yelled, "OUT AT FIRST BASE!" We ended the game with a triple play and won 6-5. We were the champions! The Illinois Intercollegiate Athletic Conference (IIAC) Champions!

Dumbo was looking at me, and I looked back at him.
You could tell he couldn't believe
that I had caught the ball,
and the game was over.

Back to Real Time

Suddenly, everything was back to regular time and motion. The umpires were all running off the field. The opposing team wasn't just quiet, they were half-dead. They couldn't believe what happened. The runner who was heading back to first was lying on his back halfway between first and second. He grabbed his hat and threw it on the ground.

Dumbo was just standing there looking at me, and I was looking back at him. You could tell he couldn't believe that I had caught the ball, and that the game was over. It seemed like we looked at each other for a long time. Finally, I gave him a big smile. I jumped in the air and yelled, "We win! We win! We win!"

The crowd went crazy, hollering and screaming. The trio was doing their cheer. The entire team ran up to Tuck on the pitcher's mound. We knocked him over, and everybody fell on the ground. We were yelling and screaming and falling all over each other, slapping each other on the back, hugging each other, jumping up and down. What a wonderful sight! The fans were yelling and congratulating each other, too. Then Coach gathered our team together.

"Boys, that was the most exciting game I've ever seen! You took all three this weekend! I'm proud of you! You are the champions! You are the 1959 IIAC Champions!"

The crowd cheered. The Animals turned the benches over. They continued to do their cheer. They were still yelling at the other team, but the team, clearly dejected, ignored them and wearily climbed on the bus without a word.

We threw our hats. We threw our bats. We threw the balls. We threw the bases. It was great! It was over! None of us wanted the winning feeling and the exhilaration to end. It didn't – we celebrated the entire weekend.

Doing Clean-Up Just Once More

Before I joined the weekend celebration, I still had to gather up all the equipment for the last time that year. I reveled in collecting the bats, balls, bases, the pitching rubber rosin bag, and the rest. I tucked them safely away in the baseball barn. As I worked, I wondered for a moment what the next year would bring. But this was no time for pondering, and I ran off to join the party.

CHAPTER EIGHTEEN

Running All the Way Home

There was nothing left for me to do Monday
except turn in my gear. I was so happy I didn't even mind
seeing old Grimes.

The Party's Over

My first year of college baseball was over, and it had been successful. I hit .333; Itch and I led the league in double plays, and we had won the conference championship game with a triple play. How sweet it was! I started dreaming of playing shortstop with the Big Guys – in the Majors. Something made me think of birds... but the thought faded away like sweet roses at summer's end.

On the academic side, I didn't do too badly – two As, three Bs, and two Cs. My mom and dad were proud but wanted me to do better next year. Meanwhile, they were happy about the winning baseball season.

There was nothing left for me to do Monday except turn in my gear. I was so happy I didn't even mind seeing old Grimes. I gave him my gear, and he congratulated me on our team winning and even told me I was a pretty good rookie. I guess he wasn't so bad after all.

I headed for the training room to say goodbye to Doc. He was doing pull-ups on the gymnastic bar.

"Hardy, you had a great game and year," he said. "As a rookie, you came through real good, and you only won the Johnson & Johnson Award a couple of times. What more could you have asked for?" I thanked him for all he had done for me that year. I opened the locker room door and went out quickly, not realizing that Dave, of "Animals" fame, was just starting to mop the floor, which was part of his scholarship job. I slipped on the wet floor and knocked over Dave's water bucket. Water spread all over the floor. Dave was standing there with a mop in his hand. He didn't say anything right away, he just stared at me with heat in his eyes. I had seen that look before – those red eyes and cheeks. He threw the mop at me and yelled, "Hardy, I'm gonna kill you! Can't you see I'm working?"

He started to come after me. I got up as quickly as I could and started running. I think he would have killed me if he would have been able to get his hands on me, but I was too fast for him. I ran out the door, and past the fountain, winking at the boy and girl under the umbrella. He was behind me. I ran past Old Main, and he was still coming. I ran past the library as he yelled, "I'M GOING TO KILL YOU WHEN I GET YOU, HARDY!"

I knew he couldn't catch me! Wow! What a time. I couldn't explain it to anybody else, but I felt great. What a great first year of college! Summer was coming but I couldn't wait for the fall quarter to start in September.

I looked back. Dave was still running after me. I ran harder. "I'M GONNA KILL YOU, YOU LITTLE PUNK!"

And I just kept running.

Made in the USA
San Bernardino, CA
17 April 2015